# Eyewitness
# FORENSIC SCIENCE

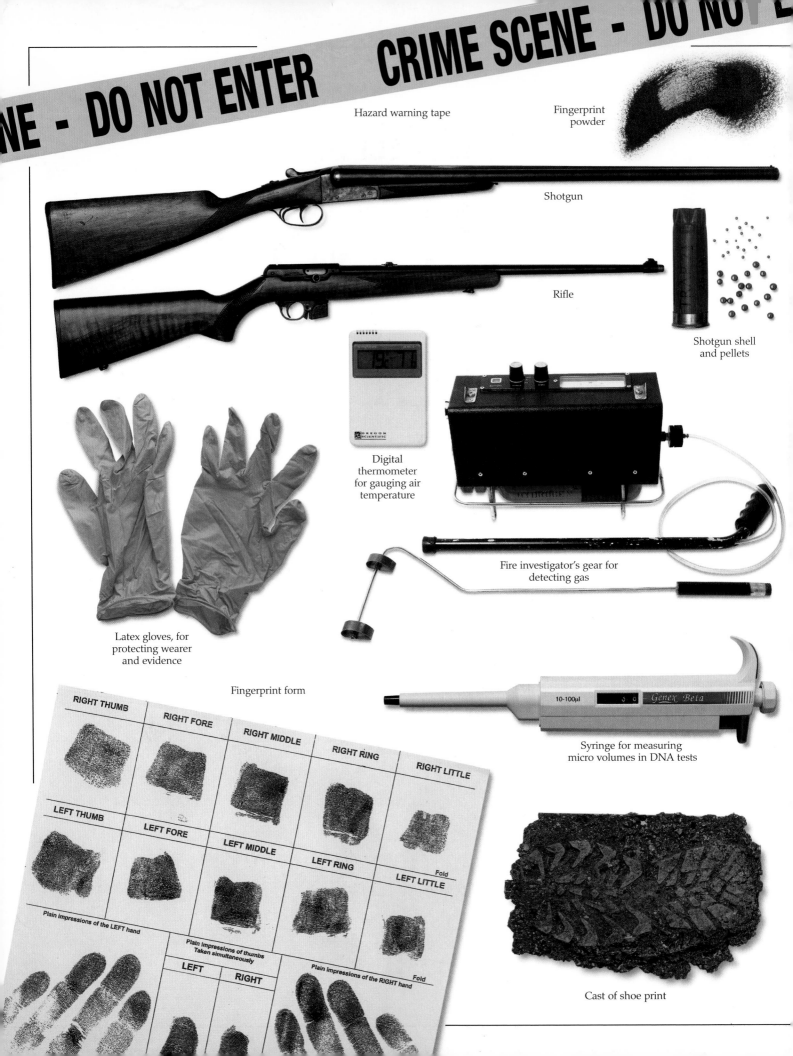

CRIME SCENE - DO NOT ENTER

...NE - DO NOT ENTER

Hazard warning tape

Fingerprint powder

Shotgun

Rifle

Shotgun shell and pellets

Digital thermometer for gauging air temperature

Fire investigator's gear for detecting gas

Latex gloves, for protecting wearer and evidence

Fingerprint form

10-100μl   Genex Beta

Syringe for measuring micro volumes in DNA tests

RIGHT THUMB

RIGHT FORE

RIGHT MIDDLE

RIGHT RING

RIGHT LITTLE

LEFT THUMB

LEFT FORE

LEFT MIDDLE

LEFT RING

LEFT LITTLE

Plain impressions of the LEFT hand

Fold

Plain impressions of thumbs
Taken simultaneously

LEFT        RIGHT

Plain impressions of the RIGHT hand

Fold

Cast of shoe print

Linen tester
for magnifying
fingerprints

# Eyewitness
# FORENSIC
# SCIENCE

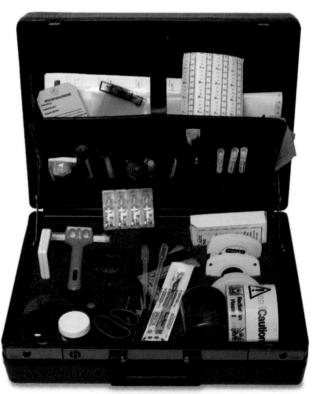

Beretta 92FS
pistol

Written by
CHRIS COOPER

Forensic investigator's toolkit

DK Publishing

Vial for DNA samples

Callipers for Bertillon
body measurements

Sniffer dog

2

Photographer's
marker card

Pipette

Scalpel

Tweezers

Fingerprint
powder brush

Camera for
photographic record

Magnetic wand

Sterile swab
and container
for sample

**DK**

LONDON, NEW YORK, MUNICH,
MELBOURNE, AND DELHI

**Consultant** Dr. Clive Steele

**Project editor** Mary Lindsay
**Art editor** Neville Graham
**Photographer** Andy Crawford
**Managing editor** Camilla Hallinan
**Managing art editor** Owen Peyton Jones
**Art director** Martin Wilson
**Publishing manager** Sunita Gahir
**Category publisher** Andrea Pinnington
**Picture researcher** Sarah Hopper
**DK picture library** Rose Horridge, Emma Shepherd
**Senior production editor** Vivianne Ridgeway
**Senior production controller** Man Fai Lau

**DK DELHI**
**Art director** Shefali Upadhyay
**Designer** Govind Mittal
**DTP designer** Harish Aggarwal

This Eyewitness ® Book has been conceived by
Dorling Kindersley Limited and Editions Gallimard.

First published in the United States in 2008 by
DK Publishing, 375 Hudson Street, New York, New York 10014

A catalog record for this book is available from the Library of Congress.

ISBN 978-0-7566-3383-7 (HC), 978-0-7566-3363-9 (Library Binding)

Color reproduction by Colourscan, Singapore.
Printed & bound in Hong Kong by Toppan Printing Company Ltd.

Discover more at
**www.dk.com**

# Contents

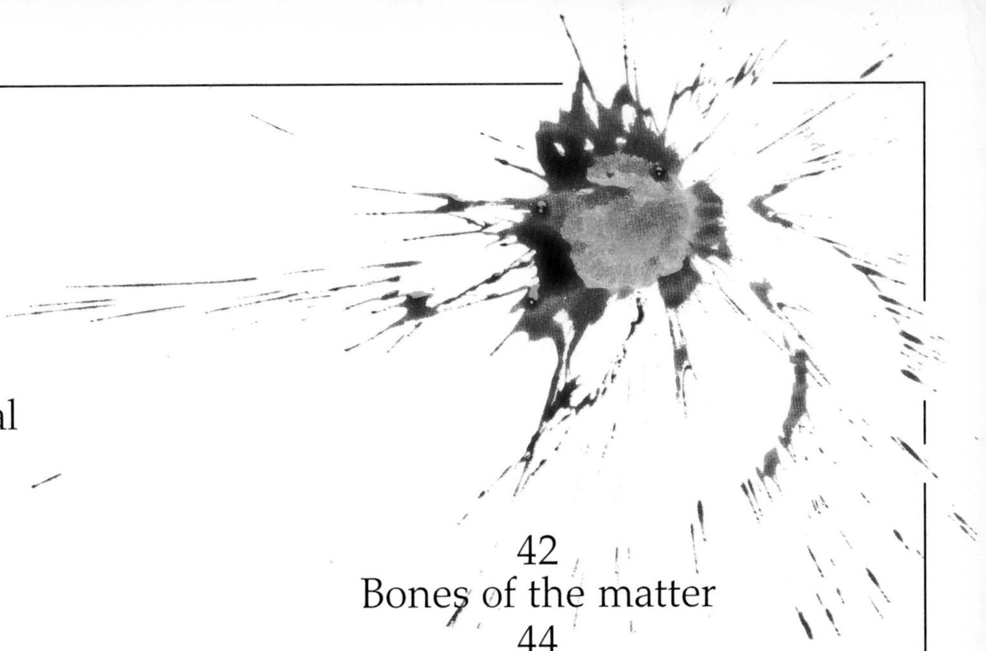

6
In pursuit of the criminal
8
The birth of forensics
10
Securing the scene
12
Recording the scene
14
Handling the evidence
16
Taking fingerprints
18
Analyzing fingerprints
20
Written in blood
22
DNA analysis
24
Trace evidence
26
Natural clues
28
A good impression
30
Guns and bullets
32
Firearms in the laboratory
34
At the scene of the crime
36
A bug's life
38
Cause of death
40
Toxic world

42
Bones of the matter
44
Spitting image
46
Behavior of the offender
48
Fire testing
50
Fire in the laboratory
52
Crash investigation
54
The big bang
56
Computer forensics
58
Paper trail
60
Every picture tells a story
62
Future forensics
64
Key people
66
Timeline of forensic firsts
69
Find out more
70
Glossary
72
Index

# In pursuit of the criminal

FORENSIC SCIENCE IS THE USE OF SCIENTIFIC methods and knowledge to investigate crime—the word "forensic" comes from the Latin *forum* and means presenting and interpreting scientific information in court. Forensic scientists study evidence at the scene of a crime and perhaps at the homes and workplaces of suspects. They study the bodies of victims. Many sciences, from chemistry to engineering to entomology (the study of insects), are used in an investigation. If there is any doubt about what has happened, forensic science provides evidence that may link a suspect to a crime or prove him or her innocent. Experts investigate not only murder, assault, and bank robbery, but also smuggling animals or people, or committing fraud on the Internet—crimes of all types.

**FORENSICS AT THE CRIME SCENE**
Forensic investigators must collect evidence as soon as possible after the crime, while it is still fresh—even if the area is unsafe and they have to work under armed guard. These investigators are examining the victim of a terrorist killing in Northern Ireland in 2000. To protect the scene from contamination they wear cleansuits, which prevent traces from their clothes or skin from fouling the evidence.

*This scientist prepares a blood sample*

**FORENSICS IN THE LABORATORY**
A scientist in a laboratory of the Federal Bureau of Investigation (FBI) searches for clues on a gun that was picked up at the scene of a crime. She looks for clues such as fingerprints or traces of blood or sweat that might identify who last used the gun. There may be signs that the gun has recently been used, or marks that show where the gun was made. The scientist may be able to identify the make of gun from the FBI's extensive database containing gun information.

*A forensic scientist tests a gun for clues*

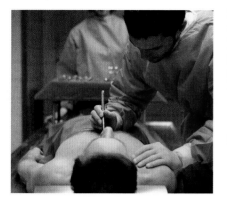

## AT AN AUTOPSY

A forensic pathologist is making an incision in the chest of a dead man. His main job is to find out the cause of death and inform the police if there are signs of a crime. After checking any external markings for clues as to the cause of death, he cuts the body open to examine the internal organs. He will remove some of them in order to inspect them closely and also to examine underlying organs and other structures, but they will all be replaced in the body before it is buried or cremated.

## FORENSICS IN COURT

At a criminal trial, it is the job of forensic scientists to provide evidence, regardless of whether it favors the prosecution or the defense. The results of the experts' painstaking work often end up in court. Here photographs made at the scene of the crime are presented in the sensational trial of the professional football player O. J. Simpson, who was accused of double murder. The defense and prosecution lawyers pitted their own forensic experts against each other. The jury doubted some of the prosecution's evidence, and the trial ended with O. J. Simpson's acquittal in October 1995.

*Forensic expert presents evidence*

*Aerial photo of location of crime scene*

*Close-up view of evidence at the crime scene*

*FBI officer talks to the press*

## FORENSICS BEFORE THE PUBLIC

An FBI officer talks at a press conference following the arrest of a suspected bank robber in New Jersey. The police rely on the forensic team behind the scene—information that goes to the press and the public must be absolutely accurate. The forensic experts' reconstruction of a crime and of the description of the suspects will play a large part in the investigation and prosecution that follow.

## FORENSICS AS ENTERTAINMENT

Greg Sanders (played by Eric Szmanda) is a junior member of the forensic team in the hit TV show *CSI: Crime Scene Investigation*. Sanders uses his enthusiasm for science to track down criminals. Despite criticisms of the ways in which the show often sensationalizes forensic work, it is credited with creating unprecedented public interest in forensic science, and has spawned *CSI: Miami* and *CSI: NY*, as well as many other competitor programs worldwide.

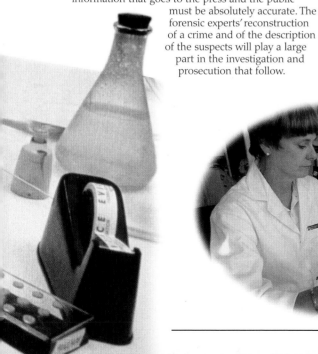

## KATHY REICHS—SCIENTIST AND NOVELIST

Forensic experts often complain that books, films, and television shows are full of inaccuracies about the scientific nature of their work. Kathy Reichs, however, brings authenticity to her best-selling thrillers, which are all written with a forensic science angle. She is a highly respected college professor who also works as a forensic scientist for US and Canadian police, specializing in the evidence that can be provided by bones. Her novels feature a forensic scientist called Temperance Brennan, whose fictional work is very similar to the writer's. A television series, *Bones*, is based on the same character.

Sliding arm of callipers to allow large measurements

# The birth of forensics

IN EARLIER TIMES, judges often thought they could tell suspects' guilt from how they behaved when confronted by accusers. They thought that a guilty person would confess under torture, while God would give an innocent person strength to resist the pain. In Europe from about the 17th century such ideas were gradually abandoned, and evidence was studied more systematically. This trend accelerated with the growth in scientific knowledge in the 19th century. Medical advances made it possible to determine causes of death more accurately. The microscope and chemical tests revealed more than ever before from evidence found at the crime scene. Precise body measurements and photographs replaced rough verbal descriptions of suspects. The first detective stories appeared, with heroes who were masters of scientific detection. These helped the public to have an understanding of the importance of science in law enforcement.

Alphonse Bertillon

### FACIAL DISCRIMINATION
An early attempt to classify human faces was made by Cesare Lombroso (1836–1909), an Italian criminologist (crime scientist). He believed that some people are born criminal and that their faces give them away. He also invented a "lie detector" that measured heart rate—lying is thought to alter heart rate.

Cesare Lombroso

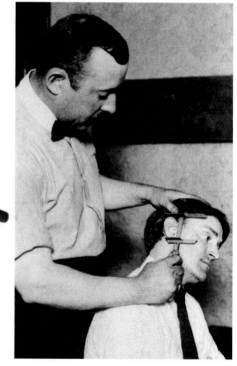

### THE POISON MAN
Mathieu Orfila (1787–1853) is called "the father of forensic toxicology"—toxicology is the study of poisons. He was called in when a woman was being tried for murdering her husband with arsenic. The poison had been found in his food, but not in his body. Orfila discovered arsenic in the man's body, and showed it did not come from the soil around the grave. The wife was jailed.

### MIRROR OF THE SOUL
A page from Lombroso's book, *The Criminal Man*, shows a selection of faces that he believed were typical of certain criminals. No. 1, for example, is an Italian bandit, while the woman is an arsonist (fire-raiser). No one now believes that you can spot a criminal just by looking at a face.

### SIZING UP THE SUSPECT
A police officer measures the size of a suspect's ear in New York in 1908, using special callipers that have one fixed and one sliding arm. This was just one of the dozens of measurements needed to build up a picture according to the Bertillon system. If this man had committed any offenses in the past, or if he ever went on the run in the future, he could be identified—though not with complete certainty—by his Bertillon measurements. However, even at the turn of the 20th century, this system was fast being replaced by the new technique of fingerprinting that had a more scientific basis.

## "MEASURING" THE PERSON

The earliest scientific system for identifying people by their physical appearance was called Bertillonage, after its French inventor Alphonse Bertillon (1853–1914). This system used measurements of the body, such as the lengths of arms and legs, the diameter of the head, and other statistics, as well as body markings such as scars or tattoos, and photographs of the suspect. Although the system was slow and cumbersome, and could not always tell people apart, it was used by many police forces for years. It suffered a blow in 1903 when an American called Will West was sent to prison, before it was discovered that another prisoner there had almost the same Bertillon measurements—and was named William West.

*Window displaying recorded measurement*

*Rule measuring centimeters*

*Small sliding arm*

## EARLY MUGSHOTS

Bertillon measurements were supplemented with photographs, which came to be called "mugshots." Usually a photograph would be taken from the side ("in profile") and from the front. If the person committed a crime at some future time, his mugshot would be widely distributed, so that he could be recognized by policemen on the beat or by the public. The profiles shown here are from just one of the many pages of Bertillon's original book of mugshots.

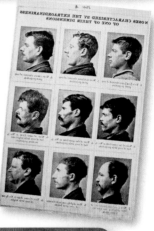

## POLICING BECOMES SCIENTIFIC

The pioneering forensic laboratory shown here was established in 1932 by the boss of the FBI, J. Edgar Hoover. Police forces began to realize that scientific principles were needed in their work. This laboratory was equipped for up-to-date tests using chemistry, physics, and engineering. Evidence began to be properly stored and protected until it could be examined. As scientific methods became more and more sensitive, so the precautions taken in collecting the evidence became greater. Today every major country has at least one advanced forensic science laboratory.

## FICTIONAL FORENSICS

Sherlock Holmes, the fictional detective created by Sir Arthur Conan Doyle, is pictured studying a piece of evidence through a powerful magnifying glass. Close at hand are a microscope and various pieces of chemical apparatus. The most famous detective in fiction made his first appearance in print in 1887. He is described as paying attention to tiny pieces of evidence that others overlooked. The character of Holmes was wildly popular—this still is from the popular 1942 film, *The Voice of Terror*.

Basil Rathbone as Holmes

## LETTER FROM THE RIPPER?

This is one of hundreds of letters—probably all hoaxes—claiming to be from the serial killer "Jack the Ripper," who terrorized London's East End in 1888. The primitive forensic methods of the time could discover little from this letter. Modern DNA testing suggests that it was from a woman. The letter is almost certainly a hoax.

# Securing the scene

IN THE PAST, policemen would walk around the scene of a crime and handle evidence with their bare hands. This didn't matter much, since the simple forensic techniques available could not detect the effects of their actions on the evidence. Today, with the enormous advances in forensic science, the situation is very different. With a serious crime, the forensic specialists turn the scene into an area resembling a laboratory. Only authorized personnel are allowed past the police warning tape. The investigators record evidence on the spot, with photographs, sketches, notes, and measurements, and then take away essential evidence—including bodies, if there are any. At the same time, police officers locate witnesses and take statements. Speed is vital: witnesses must be questioned while memories are still fresh, and physical evidence must be preserved before it is altered by time or weather conditions. This precious window of opportunity is known as the "golden hour."

**BY INVITATION ONLY**
One of the first things the police do when they arrive at the scene of a crime is to make sure no one is in danger. Their next priority is to get help to anyone who has been injured. Then they cordon off the area. Curious onlookers, journalists, and cameramen often crowd around the scene of a crime. It is imperative to keep them away until the evidence has been collected. This is to ensure that they do not accidentally contaminate the scene and mislead investigators. Only authorized police officers are allowed to cross the line.

*One member of the team takes notes*

*The forensic photographer makes a record of the scene*

# DO NOT ENTER

# CRIME SCENE - DO

## BEFORE THE TRAIL GOES COLD

If a body found at an incident shows signs of life, the person must be rushed to the hospital. If not, it must be certified dead by a qualified medical examiner before it is moved. This body was found in the aftermath of Hurricane Katrina in New Orleans in 2005. A forensic investigation was needed because the police couldn't assume that every body found was a victim of the hurricane and not of a crime committed some time before the hurricane struck.

## FIRST ANSWER

Many crime investigations depend on a few facts among many thousands of items of information provided by people living near the scene of a crime. The whole area may be flooded with police officers asking the same carefully devised questions from a checklist. In addition, the police may be equipped with visual cues, such as photographs or drawings of victims or suspects. Such an enormous effort in terms of manpower and time can only be put into the most serious of crimes.

## PLANE CRASH SCENE

Crash investigators study the scattered wreckage of an airliner that caught fire on landing at Yogyakarta, Indonesia. The cause of a disaster like this is usually discovered only after a long and painstaking investigation carried out by experts at the scene. Many questions must be asked: was it an accident or a crime? Was the airline negligent, or was the aircrew careless? Did someone sabotage the plane?

## FINGERTIP SEARCH

A line of police officers wearing "cleansuits" advances on hands and knees, searching every square inch of a road. The body of a murdered woman was found nearby, and there could be signs of the killer's arrival or departure. Similarly thorough searches for clues may need to be made in the surrounding countryside, in streets, or through people's household waste. In many crimes, the searchers don't know what they're looking for. Although the vast majority of the objects found are not relevant to the investigation they still have to be cataloged and treated as potential evidence until events prove they have no part to play.

*Search on hands and knees ensures no evidence is missed*

## SEARCH PATTERNS

There are many equally good patterns in which an area can be searched. Sticking to one pattern ensures the best cover of ground in the shortest possible time. The pattern of search should leave no area out, and preferably should cover each point twice, but shouldn't waste effort by searching the same area more than that. It should be directed by a single person to avoid any confusion.

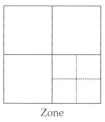

Spiral

Grid

Line

Zone

# Recording the scene

WHEN FORENSIC INVESTIGATORS arrive at a crime scene, they make a permanent record of anything that is relevant to the crime. They write descriptions of what they see, draw diagrams, and take photographs. Not only does all this scrupulous care and attention to fine detail avoid having to rely on highly unreliable human memory, it also provides evidence that is likely to be accepted in a court. The investigators also behave according to a principle stated by the French forensics pioneer Edmond Locard: "Every contact leaves a trace." This means that everyone who visits a crime scene leaves microscopic traces of material—hairs, sweat, flakes of skin, fibers from their clothes, or soil from their shoes. He or she also carries away traces from the scene—dust, pollen, grease from a gun, fibers from a carpet or upholstery, or traces of drugs or explosives. The principle applies equally to the police and forensics experts at the scene—and so they take every precaution to make sure they do not contaminate the site by always wearing protective clothing and footwear.

Vital clue—dried blood on a brick

*Hood to keep hair in place*

*Face mask in case of noxious substances*

*All-in-one protective cleansuit*

## FORENSIC FASHION

The "cleansuits" worn by forensic officers prevent particles, fibers, sweat, and dirt from passing from the investigators onto items of evidence. The work of the scientists would be made much harder if the evidence they were analyzing consisted of, for example, hair from one of the investigators, or soil that they had walked into the area. The cleansuits also help to prevent contamination if there is poison or infectious germs at the scene. Special "overshoes" with "POLICE" embossed in mirror writing on the soles ensure that the team's footprints are not confused with those belonging to the suspects.

## CAPTURING THE SCENE

A forensic photographer, who wears a cleansuit just like all the other officers, records a suspicious object—a knife—at the crime scene. He photographs the crime scene from every angle, so that investigators do not have to rely on their memories or the sketches as they reconstruct the events that happened there. Often the photographer includes a scale in the photograph so that people viewing the picture at a later date have a clear idea of the size of the object.

## PORTRAIT OF THE CRIME

An investigator's drawing of the crime scene shows where a body has been found, possibly the victim of a murder. The sketch also marks the positions of objects and the distances between them, and notes any peculiarities that a photograph does not bring out. The officer may use a handheld computer to aid in rapidly producing a high-quality diagram. The sketch is signed as a true record of the scene.

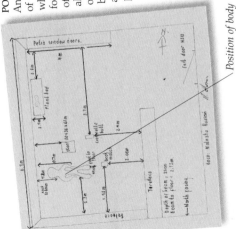

*Position of body*

*Equipment case*

*Overshoe*

*Sole of shoe marked "POLICE" in raised letters*

*Glove to protect skin and to preserve evidence from contamination*

### THE SHAPE OF DEATH
Whenever a body is found at a crime scene, its outline is drawn on the floor, if found inside, or the ground outside. Only when the position of the body has been marked and the body photographed extensively from many different angles can it be removed. The position of the body might give clues about an attack, or show that a suspect's story is not accurate. In the scene above, a nearby stain of blood that has leaked from the body is also marked.

### STATIC PLATE
Forensic investigators use static plates such as this one when it is important to keep from disturbing the ground or stepping on important clues. They move from spot to spot, putting static plates down at each place.

### KEEPING TRACK
Footprints can provide all manner of useful information but they have a short lifespan. However, a copy, or cast, can be made to provide a permanent and transportable record. This is done by filling the print with liquid plaster of Paris or "dental stone" (a material used by dentists to make teeth molds) and allowing it to set hard. The low frame around the print seals off the area while the cast material sets. If the print has been made on an extremely soft surface such as snow, it can be sprayed with a material that makes it firmer before attempting to make a cast of the print.

*Scale to measure size of footprint*

*Footprint in damp sand*

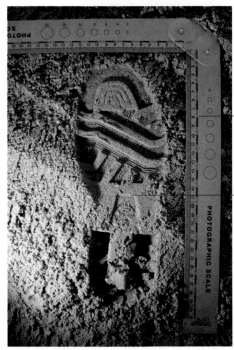

*Plaster of Paris*

### MARKER CARDS
When investigators take photographs, they identify important objects in the crime scene by placing marker cards in position. The cards are numbered (or lettered) and a list of the numbers (letters) and the features being referred to is made. Later, investigators, lawyers, and witnesses can refer back to these objects and places with less risk of confusing vital information or of omitting it.

*Card marking the fifteenth piece of evidence*

15

# Handling the evidence

An incident scene is a hive of activity as forensic investigators record and collect all the evidence that could possibly be relevant. Having taken great care—by wearing cleansuits, gloves, and overshoes—not to contaminate anything, the investigators must take equal care that no one and nothing else can damage the evidence during the course of its life, which is often long. Anything removed from the site goes into a container that is sealed and labeled. Seals on bags and bottles are "tamper evident," showing obvious signs if they've been opened. Containers carry "progress-of-custody" labels—each person who handles the evidence signs the label so a court has confidence in its contents.

**1. Fingerprint forms—**
*prints are inked onto these*

### TOOLKIT
There is no time to lose at the scene of a crime or other incident—all the investigator's tools must be ready and on hand. Evidence that needs to be preserved is put into bags, bottles, or envelopes. Blood and other fluids are gathered on swabs resembling household cotton swabs. Adhesive tape and scissors are handy. Many items in the toolkit are disposable—gloves, scalpels, and other things cannot be used again in case they contaminate the evidence. Containers are sealed, and labels track their movements.

**2. Labels** *to attach to items of evidence*

**3. Lifting tape** *to "capture" fingerprints on objects*

**4. Fingerprint brushes** *for applying powder to fingerprints*

### PHOTOGRAPHIC RECORD
Crime-scene investigators normally use film cameras like this one. Digital images are sometimes challenged in court on the grounds that it is easy to alter them, but ways of guarding against this are being developed. As soon as full protection against tampering is possible, the use of digital photography in forensics is set to increase.

**5. Vials** *of pure water to dissolve dried stains*

**6. Roller** *for pressing lifting tape onto fingerprints*

### MEASURING SCALES
Forensic investigators carry various scales (rulers). Scientists measure objects at the scene and place scales next to objects being photographed to show their size. These right-angled scales can be placed inside a corner—of a room, for example—or outside corners—of furniture, for example—to provide quick and easy readings.

**7. Digital thermometer** *measures air temperature at scene*

## BAGS OF EVIDENCE

Every piece of evidence—however large or small—that is found at the scene of an incident must be placed in a tamper-proof evidence bag. Such bags come in many designs and sizes—they may be made of paper with the contents hidden, or of plastic through which the evidence is visible. But all evidence bags have a printed area in which all handlers of the bag have to give their details. This "chain of custody" ensures that important evidence remains exactly the same as it was when first found.

Transparent evidence bag

**8. Magnifying glass**

**9. Tweezers** *to pick up small objects*

**10. Protractor** *to measure angles*

**11. Aluminum fingerprint powder** *to make fingerprints visible*

**12. Magnetic fingerprint poweder** *to make fingerprints visible*

**13. Disposable rulers**

**14. Swabs in vials** *to collect samples of fluids*

**15. Latex gloves**

**16. Measuring tapes**

**17. Scalpel,** *a disposable knife*

**18. Hazard warning tapes** *to be placed around areas to be protected*

**19. Pipettes** *for moving drops of liquid*

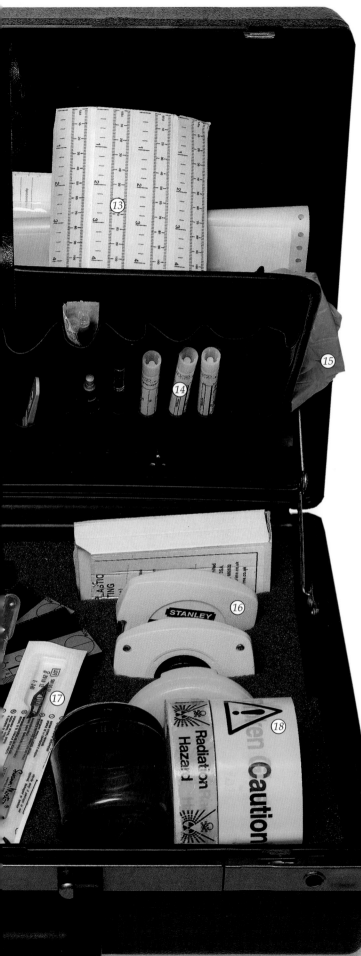

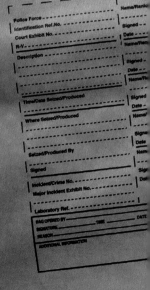

Paper evidence bag

POLICE EVI

Police Force
Identification Ref.No.
Court Exhibit No.
R-V
Description

Name/Rank
Signed
Date
Name/Ren
Signed
Date
Name/Re

Time/Date Seized/Produced
Where Seized/Produced
Seized/Produced By
Signed
Incident/Crime No.
Major Incident Exhibit No.
Laboratory Ref.

BAG OPENED BY
SIGNATURE
REASON
ADDITIONAL INFORMATION

TIME
DATE

# Taking fingerprints

THE FIRST POLICE FORCE to collect and store fingerprints systematically to identify criminals was in Argentina, in the 1890s. Today, every country keeps a store of criminals' fingerprints. Forensic investigators try to find all the fingerprints at a crime scene. A print that is visible to the naked eye is called a patent print; one that appears invisible but can be made visible is a latent print. The investigators make permanent copies of the prints and photograph them. Prints are taken from everyone known to have been at the scene—including, for example, family members—so that they can be compared with those of suspects or people whose prints are held on file as a result of some earlier misconduct.

**DUSTING FOR PRINTS**
A police officer brushes fingerprint dust onto a car door. A smooth, metal surface readily takes fingerprints. Since cars come in many colors, investigators need a range of colors of fingerprint powder, so that they can choose contrasting ones to show up the prints. There are an enormous number of places in a car where prints might be found—the interior, the exterior body, the engine compartment, the trunk, and even perhaps underneath the car.

**THE WIDER VIEW**
The magnifying glass is one of the oldest and simplest aids for the detective, but still one of the most valuable. It is indispensable for getting a better view of fingerprints, significant marks and scratches, and small writing and printing.

**BRUSHES**
The fingerprint specialist uses brushes to cover areas where prints are visible or suspected with a fine powder. Sweeping away the excess leaves the pattern of the print revealed in the dust. A broad brush cleans larger areas; a narrower brush can be pushed into recesses. The type of brush also depends on the type of powder chosen.

**FINGERPRINT POWDER**
A small heap of fingerprint powder left after an investigator has taken a brushful to spread on a fingerprint. The consistency and color of the powder is chosen depending on the type of surface being checked. Dark fingerprint powder usually consists of fine particles of carbon, rather like soot. Light powders may be chalk, titanium dioxide, or other materials.

**LIFTING TAPE**
This clear adhesive tape can be pressed onto a surface carrying a fingerprint so that the print is transferred onto it. The print can then be removed for analysis and comparison with known prints on file.

**ROLLER**
A fingerprint roller is used to smooth lifting tape onto a fingerprint. The pressure from forcing the roller over the tape removes air bubbles and allows optimum contact between tape and print to make an accurate impression.

## PROCEDURE FOR TAKING FINGERPRINTS

Fingerprint specialists have to know where to look for prints, how to dust an invisible or damaged print so that it produces a clear and accurate image, and how to preserve it so that it can be used as evidence, possibly years later. Brushing the surface with carbon powder is still the most widely used method.

**1 BRUSHING THE SURFACE**
The fingerprints on this dish are barely visible. To show them up, fingerprint powder is brushed lightly over the surface with a brush. The investigator is careful to wear gloves.

**2 REVEALING THE PRINT**
A large print is now clearly visible on the surface of the object. However, to make it into a piece of evidence that can be used it needs to be made much clearer and more permanent.

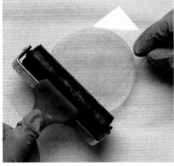

**3 USING THE ROLLER**
The investigator lays lifting tape over the surface and runs the roller over it, pressing down firmly so that some of the grease making up the fingerprint is transferred to the film.

**4 COPYING THE PRINT**
The forensic scientist peels back the lifting tape away from the surface of the dish, being careful to do it in one smooth motion. The tape now carries its copy of the fingerprint.

**5 FATE OF THE FINGERPRINT**
The print on the lifting film is placed in a protective sleeve with a label recording when and where it was obtained. It may be examined visually (as here), photographed, or scanned electronically. Its details end up in a computer database, while the physical fingerprint is safely stored.

## WAVING A WAND

A magnetic wand used with metal dust is an alternative to a brush used with nonmetallic powders. The fine dust of metal filings forms a bushy clump at one end of the wand. The fingerprint officer uses the wand to brush the dust onto the area being studied, and some of the metal sticks to the grease of the print pattern and produces a recordable print.

### MAGNETIC POWDER
Magnetic powder contains iron so that it is attracted by magnets. It comes in many colors but cannot be used on iron, steel, and many other kinds of metal.

*Magnetic tip attracts filings*

**1 GATHERING DUST**
An investigator inserts the wand into the magnetic fingerprint dust and lifts a mass of dust on the tip of the magnetic wand. The dust forms a natural "brush" that has little chance of damaging a fingerprint.

Large magnetic wand    Smaller pen-size magnetic wand

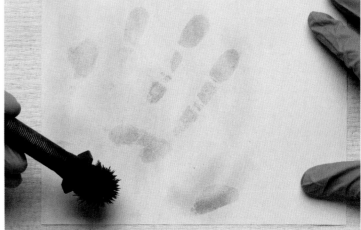

**2 MAKING CONTACT WITH THE PRINT**
Gentle brushing of the magnetic dust over the surface shows up a large part of a hand. Normally only fingerprints are kept on file, but hand markings are also unique to each person and can be a useful addition to the evidence. One of the advantages of magnetic dust is that the excess is easily removed with the wand, more easily than ordinary dust is removed with an ordinary brush. This allows a cleaner print to be prepared in a shorter space of time.

# Analyzing fingerprints

For hundreds of years people occasionally commented on the fact that people's fingerprints—the patterns of looped and branching ridges on the fingertips—differ from person to person. It was not until the mid-19th century that they were first used by British officials in India in place of signatures on contracts. Then the British scientist Francis Galton published his studies of fingerprints, showing two crucial facts: that everyone's prints are different, and that everyone's prints stay the same through the whole of their lives. In 1891, Argentina started to make use of fingerprints; British and American police forces soon followed. Now every country has records of fingerprints and has police trained in collecting and analyzing them. Storage and analysis of fingerprints are computerized these days, and fingerprint information can be flashed between police forces around the world in a matter of seconds. Palmprints and footprints are also unique, and sometimes these are used to identify people, too.

**SIR WILLIAM HERSCHEL**
In the mid-19th century Herschel (1833–1918), a British official in India, started demanding that the local people put their palmprints on legal documents as a way of showing their agreement. Later he refined this to just requiring the marks of two fingerprints. At first he simply wanted to encourage the people to respect the authority of the document, but he soon came to realize that fingerprints were also unique individual identifiers.

**QUICK PRINTING**
Fingerprint specialists often use ready-inked pieces of film to speed up the process of taking fingerprints. When the protective layer has been peeled off, the witness or suspect presses each of his or her fingertips onto the ink. In turn, each fingerprint is transferred onto a specially printed fingerprint form. This ensures a consistency of recording that makes comparing prints easier.

*Each finger of each hand has an individual and distinctive appearance*

*Pre-inked paper has made print taking quicker and less messy*

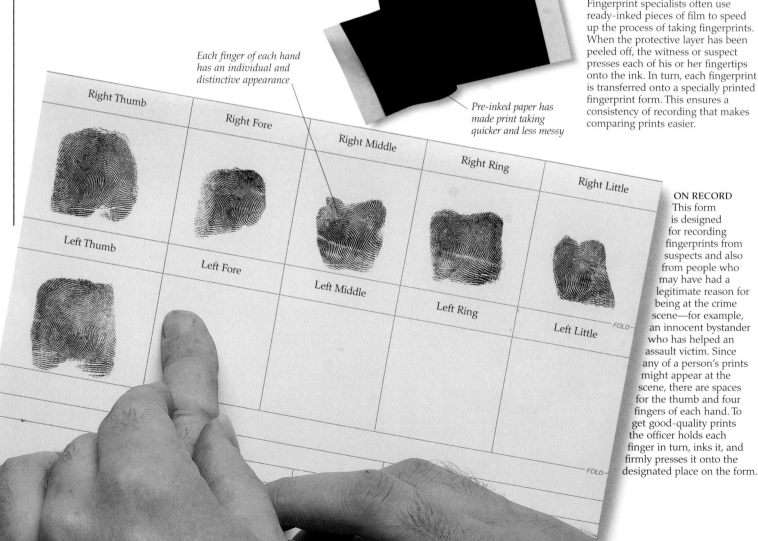

Right Thumb · Right Fore · Right Middle · Right Ring · Right Little
Left Thumb · Left Fore · Left Middle · Left Ring · Left Little

FOLD

**ON RECORD**
This form is designed for recording fingerprints from suspects and also from people who may have had a legitimate reason for being at the crime scene—for example, an innocent bystander who has helped an assault victim. Since any of a person's prints might appear at the scene, there are spaces for the thumb and four fingers of each hand. To get good-quality prints the officer holds each finger in turn, inks it, and firmly presses it onto the designated place on the form.

FOLD

## PATTERNS OF PRINTS

The three pictures below show the most common fingerprint patterns. The details within each pattern are what the experts look at to determine similarity. In whorls, the ridges near the center of the pattern form closed curves. Loops are the most common type of print; each ridge enters and leaves on the right or left side of the finger. In an arch, each ridge enters and leaves on opposite sides.

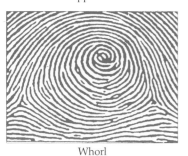

Whorl

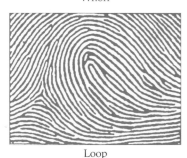

Loop

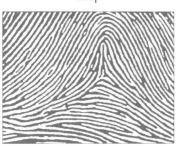

Arch

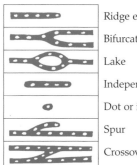

Ridge ending

Bifurcation

Lake

Independent ridge

Dot or island

Spur

Crossover

## GALTON DETAILS

When they are comparing prints, fingerprint officers look at tiny features (listed above) that appear on the ridges. These are called Galton's details, after Sir Francis Galton (1822–1911), the fingerprint pioneer. The expert looks at where the details occur, and if there are many identical details he or she declares the two prints to come from the same person.

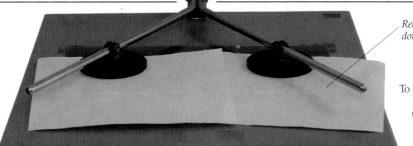

*Recorded prints upside down on comparator*

## MATCHING THE PRINTS

To compare two fingerprints to find out if they are the same, the expert needs to have them side by side. The two images are placed on top of this comparator, which enlarges and projects them in the two windows at the front. The expert looks first for the main features—loops, whorls, arches—and then at the Galton details—the ways in which the ridges end, branch, or form tiny loops. The main patterns are often crossed by cracks in the skin or tiny scars that occur through wear and tear and can change the print's appearance. The expert disregards these.

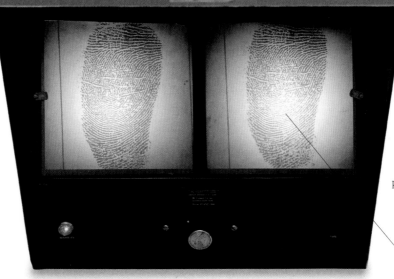

*Magnification of fingerprint on screen to highlight details*

*Can suspended in glue vapor*

## VISUALIZING FINGERPRINTS

A hard-to-see fingerprint can be made more visible by "super-glue fuming." The object—a can, in this case—is put in a cabinet with a small amount of a super-gluelike substance. When heated, the glue gives off fumes that react with the grease in the print. This forms a hard opaque deposit that is easy to see.

## SHINING A LIGHT ON CRIME

Finding a fingerprint is one thing but getting a clear enough copy to be able to analyze it in detail is quite another matter. One way to help improve the quality of a print is to use laser light rather than ordinary light. Laser can often show up faint details more clearly. Here, it is shone on the can treated in the super-glue fuming process at left. The fingerprints have already been made clearer by the super-glue treatment that has now coated the can in a hard deposit. The laser light shows up the prints even more clearly. The prints will be photographed, and the can will also be kept as a permanent record until the crime is cleared up.

*Fingerprint shown up by glue fuming*

## COMPUTERIZED MATCHING

A fingerprint expert in Taiwan compares the fingerprint image held in his left hand with two images on a computer screen. The handheld image is from the scene of a recent crime; the computer versions are from records of known criminals, which are held on a database. The original analysis of the electronic prints after they were first taken was largely carried out by computer. Computers can store and quickly process a lot of data, but human experts are involved at every stage, and only the human eye is capable of confirming the final match.

# Written in blood

In PAST TIMES, blood was not a very useful clue in a crime. If a farmer's clothes had a suspicious stain on them, for example, he could claim it was an animal's blood. A carpenter might say the stain was paint. But in the late 19th century, chemical tests were invented that could show whether a stain was blood or not. A very useful one that is still used as a quick, scene-of-the-crime test is the Kastle-Meyer test, but it cannot tell human from animal blood. Around 1900, Paul Uhlenhuth invented a chemical test that had to be performed in a laboratory; this showed whether blood was human. Since then, more sophisticated ways of analyzing blood have been invented. They may even show how the person died—if, for example, by poison or suffocation.

**KARL LANDSTEINER**
Around 1902, Dr. Karl Landsteiner (1868–1943) showed that there are several different types, or groups, of blood. This explained why blood transfusions were so often unsuccessful in those days: a patient can only receive blood of certain groups. In police work, if two bloodstains are of different groups, it follows that they must come from different people.

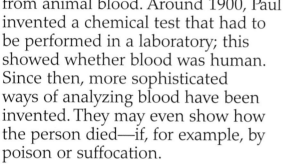

*Blood sample*    *Reagent (chemical used for testing)*

**JOHN GLAISTER**
John Glaister (1892–1971) classified bloodstains into six types, according to their shape, which depended on how they were produced. Much the same classification is still in use today. Glaister and his father were professors of forensic medicine, showing that the subject had been accepted as an important area of science by the latter part of the 19th century.

**TESTING KIT**
The rows numbered 1–4 hold samples of the main blood groups: A, B, O, and AB. Reagents are added to reveal the blood group. For example, in the left-hand column, anti-A reagent makes A and AB form a clot, which proves the existence of A antigens, while B and O remain liquid as they contain no A antigens.

**KASTLE-MEYER TEST**
The quick blood tests that investigators can do at the scene of the crime are called "presumptive" tests. The most common is the Kastle-Meyer test. If the test rules out a fluid or a stain as being blood, no further tests are needed. However, if it indicates that the stain or mark could be blood, more sensitive and specific tests must be carried out in a laboratory for confirmation. That detailed investigation will also reveal whether the blood is human or animal, what its group is, whether it shows signs of disease, and much more.

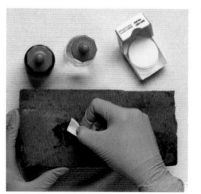

**1 REMOVING A TRACE**
A stain that has been found on a brick near the site of a crime is suspected to be dried human blood. The investigator rubs it with the corner of a disk of paper that has been folded into four in order to collect a sample consisting of just a few grains.

**2 CHECKING THE SAMPLE**
The disk of paper is unfolded, and the sample is clearly seen as a dot at its centre. The investigator wears gloves not only to protect the sample from contamination but also to protect the investigator from contamination from disease-bearing fluids.

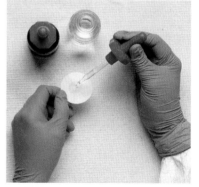

**3 ADDING REAGENT**
The investigator adds a few drops of a chemical reagent called phenolphthalein from a dropper onto the sample. The test is so sensitive that only a small quantity of the chemical is needed.

## PATTERNS OF BLOODSTAINS

The shape that bloodstains make at the scene of an incident can give valuable information about their cause—whether they came spurting from an artery or whether they were the result of slower bleeding from smaller blood vessels, whether the victim was moving at the time, or whether the injury was caused by a blow, a knife wound, or in some other way. In the 1930s, Sir John Glaister classified bloodstains into six main types: drops; splashes; pools; spurts; smears; and trails. However, many factors can influence the shapes, and an expert has to be very cautious in his or her interpretation.

*Blood is smeared over a large area*

*Point from which blood trails radiate*

## BLOOD SMEAR

The blood smear (left) is the result of a quantity of blood being spread over a surface, either by the injured person trying to get away from the scene, or by the person falling as he or she dies. A blood smear may also be caused by the victim being moved from or within the crime scene, either at the time of the injury or soon afterward. There is plenty of blood here from which investigators can take one or more samples for testing.

## IMPACT SPLATTER

When a bloodstain found on the floor or ground splatters out from a central area, as in the picture above, it is a sign that the blood has fallen from a height. It is possible to estimate how far the blood has fallen, which can give the investigators certain information about the height of the victim, or about his or her location at the time of the attack.

## SHOE PRINT

If there has been a very violent incident, with much blood shed, it is unlikely that anyone will leave the scene unmarked. Here, an excellent blood print of the sole pattern of a shoe has been left near the scene of the crime. In addition to giving clues to the size and make of shoe, the print shows some defects that may link it uniquely to its wearer.

## TEARDROP SHAPE

Blood stains are often teardrop-shaped. Sometimes this is a result of a spherical drop flying through the air and spreading as it strikes a surface. This can give valuable clues about the movement of the victim as he or she was wounded. In other stains, such as this one, the teardrop shape is due to gravity forcing the blood downward.

## CIRCULAR DROP

When a drop of blood is circular in shape, it indicates that it struck the surface at right angles— usually by falling vertically onto a floor. However, there is still a possibility that the victim was moving, even if very slowly.

*Bloodied fingerprint*

## FINGERPRINT

A fingerprint in blood is two pieces of evidence in one. But it is possible for the fingerprint to have come from the criminal and the blood to have come from the victim—or even vice versa. To discover the truth, scrupulous testing and analysis are essential.

*More blood on intact side of shoe*

*Sole's wear and tear causes less blood here*

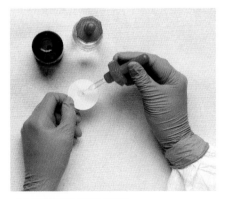

## 4 A SECOND CHEMICAL

The investigator then adds a few drops of hydrogen peroxide, a clear liquid that is often used as a household bleach or disinfectant. The combination of this chemical and phenolphthalein in the presence of even a minute quantity of blood causes an effect that is visible to the naked eye.

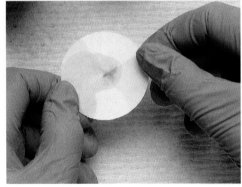

## 5 BLOOD REVEALED

The paper turns a bright pink in the area where the stain has mixed with the chemicals. This means the stain is likely to be blood. After confirmation, the sample will most likely be taken to a laboratory for more detailed tests.

# DNA analysis

A **REVOLUTION IN FORENSICS** has been brought about by DNA typing, or "genetic fingerprinting." DNA (deoxyribonucleic acid) is the substance at the heart of every human cell. It carries genetic (inherited) instructions about how our bodies are built. It controls the way a baby is going to grow up—its sex and height, hair color, and susceptibility to certain diseases. DNA molecules are spiraling chains of atoms, packed into the center of every cell. Only identical twins, triplets, and so on have the same DNA. A single hair, a drop of blood, or a smear of saliva at the scene of a crime can reveal who the criminal was—provided the DNA is stored on a database and a match is made. A criminal can wear gloves to keep from leaving fingerprints, but it is hard not to leave any DNA.

## SAMPLE TO PROFILE
These vials (small bottles) contain samples of DNA that have been prepared to go through a multistep DNA typing process. Samples may be taken from the scene of a crime— for example, from a blood stain—and from suspects, usually taken from cells scraped from inside the cheek. The test can show whether the crime-scene samples come from one individual or more than one, and whether the suspect is the same person as the person at the scene.

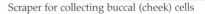
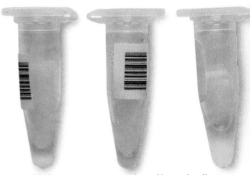

Scraper for collecting buccal (cheek) cells

Vials containing samples of buccal cells

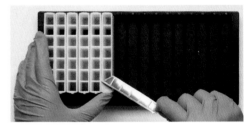

### 1 TRANSFERRING THE DNA
A scientist picks up some of the contents of the first vial and drops it into the first compartment of a multipart container. (Six containers are visible here.) She uses a pipette, or dropper, that has a digital scale showing the precise amount that she drops in. She repeats the process for the first compartment in each of the six containers.

### 2 PREPARING TO PURIFY
The first compartment of each container now holds a different DNA sample. The investigator peels the foil off the six containers, ready for the purification process. The other compartments hold chemicals. In the process about to begin, reactions will take place in each compartment in turn.

## PIONEERS OF DNA
Pictured right are the two scientists who first worked out the structure of the enormously complicated DNA molecule. All living matter contains DNA—it is the chemical blueprint of life. Francis Crick (1916–2004) (far right) and James Watson (b. 1928) discovered that DNA is in the form of a double strand. Each strand is a helix (similar to a spiral staircase) and consists of about 100 million chemical units (bases). Each base is a small group of atoms. A small fraction of the bases are "instructions" for the organism. The rest has no known function—but it's what is used in "genetic fingerprinting."

## SIR ALEC JEFFREYS
Alec Jeffreys invented DNA typing, or genetic fingerprinting in 1984. It was first used to investigate two murders committed in 1983 and 1986. A young man had confessed to both murders and had been charged, but he appeared to have the wrong type of blood. Jeffreys was able to show that the two murders had been committed by the same person, but that it was not the man who had confessed. Eventually, the DNA evidence showed that another man was the killer. In the first police use of DNA testing, Jeffreys had proved the innocence of one man and the guilt of another.

### 3 EXTRACTING AND PURIFYING
The scientist adds further chemicals (in the blue containers). The machine will automatically mix each DNA sample with the chemicals in the next compartment, then mix the results of this reaction with the next batch of chemicals, and so on. These processes extract and purify the DNA.

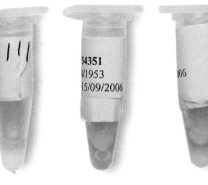

## COMPARING PROFILES

The DNA profile for each sample is a pattern in which selected fragments of the DNA, called STRs (short tandem repeats), are spread out according to their sizes. There is more than one way of showing a DNA profile: the graphs below have been produced by electrophoresis. No two people have exactly the same peaks, or spikes, in the same positions in such a graph.

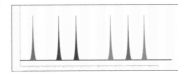

**CRIME SAMPLE**
A DNA sample from the scene can be compared with samples taken from various suspects.

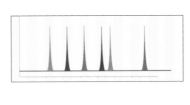

**VICTIM SAMPLE**
The victim's DNA may be at the crime scene, and must not be confused with the offender's.

**ENDANGERED SPECIES**
The parrots, macaws, hummingbirds, and other species in this print are just some of the rich array of birds of Central and South America. Their survival is threatened by illegal trading to countries where the demand for exotic pets flourishes. Traveling long distances in atrocious conditions leads to many casualties. Often the only way the authorities have of identifying smuggled birds and other animals is to analyze the DNA from their remains. DNA analysis can also confirm where the animal originally come from. If it belongs to a protected species, prison or a heavy fine can follow.

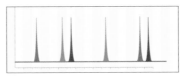

**FIRST SUSPECT**
This shows some peaks like those of the crime sample, but others, too. It can be ruled out.

## 4 AMPLIFYING THE DNA

The next step in this complex process is to "amplify" the DNA—increase its amount by making copies of the molecules, and copies of the copies, repeatedly. This machine runs the samples through a multistep process called PCR (polymerase chain reaction), which doubles the number of molecules at each step. After doing this many times there may be hundreds of thousands of times as much DNA as there was to start with. Amplifying the DNA ensures that there is enough material for the scientists to work with.

**SECOND SUSPECT**
This DNA pattern matches the crime sample. This suspect was at the crime scene.

**RELATIVELY GUILTY**
In 2003, two drunk men on a highway overpass in the UK threw bricks into the traffic. One smashed through a truck windshield, causing the driver to have a heart attack. Some of the criminal's blood was on the brick, but the DNA was not on the national DNA database. The search was widened to look for similar DNA. A man who was on the database because he had a criminal conviction had very similar DNA. The man's brother proved to be guilty.

## 5 CREATING THE PROFILE

Finally, the multiplied DNA samples are placed in an electrophoresis machine. Inside, a strong electric field of hundreds of volts drags the fragments of DNA along a thin tube called a capillary, separating them out according to the size of the fragments. The positions of the fragments are detected electronically and used to generate visible patterns or sequences of numbers. These form the DNA profiles of the person or people from whom the original DNA samples came.

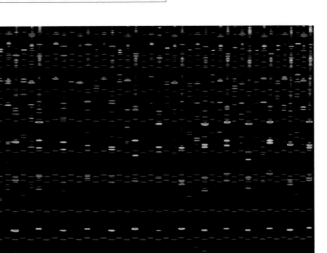

**DNA PROFILES**
The DNA profiles of several people are compared above. Through a series of complex chemical processes, even minute traces of a person's DNA can be displayed in this graphic way. This helps the forensic expert to make comparisons with other samples. DNA databases, which are maintained in most countries around the world, hold DNA records of offenders, whatever their crime or conviction. When a crime is committed, DNA from the scene of the crime is collected and compared with profiles that exist on the database. As the databases increase in size and sophistication, more matches are being made, even concerning crimes committed many years ago.

# Trace evidence

(see p. 12)

FOLLOWING DR. EDMOND LOCARD'S exchange principle that "every contact leaves a trace" (see p. 12), forensic scientists study some very tiny traces indeed. They look for details that are too small to see with the naked eye. Often they use comparison microscopes, which are set up to look at two things at once. They also use scanning electron microscopes. Instead of beams of light, these scan objects with beams of tiny particles called electrons. Electrons are small particles that are found inside atoms. Studied at this level of detail, hairs that are apparently identical when viewed with the naked eye reveal very different surface textures. Flakes of paint from a car are seen to consist of multiple layers, with differences in thickness and color. If the flake looks identical under the electron microscope to a sample from a suspect car, it almost certainly came from that car.

### VACUUM EVIDENCE
Forensic investigators use a specially designed type of vacuum cleaner to collect fibers, dust, and other trace evidence from furniture, carpets, curtains, clothing, and car interiors. The very small nozzle makes it possible to pick up fibers from otherwise inaccessible areas.

### PAINT EFFECTS
A forensic scientist examines a sample of paint under an optical microscope and compares it with the vast range of samples in the foreground. This traditional method of examining paint can be used to compare color and type, for example, whether it is glossy or matte, oil- or water-based. With a scanning electron microscope, however, an investigator can see much more.

### COMPARISON MICROSCOPE
When samples are compared, it is best done side by side so that differences and similarities show up clearly. There are various types of comparison microscope that present the two samples in the same field of view. In this design, there are two identical microscopes, each with binocular eyepieces (eyepieces for both eyes). The samples can be viewed separately by each person looking through the eyepieces one at a time. Alternatively, the images can be transmitted through cables to a TV screen, where they can be viewed more easily side by side.

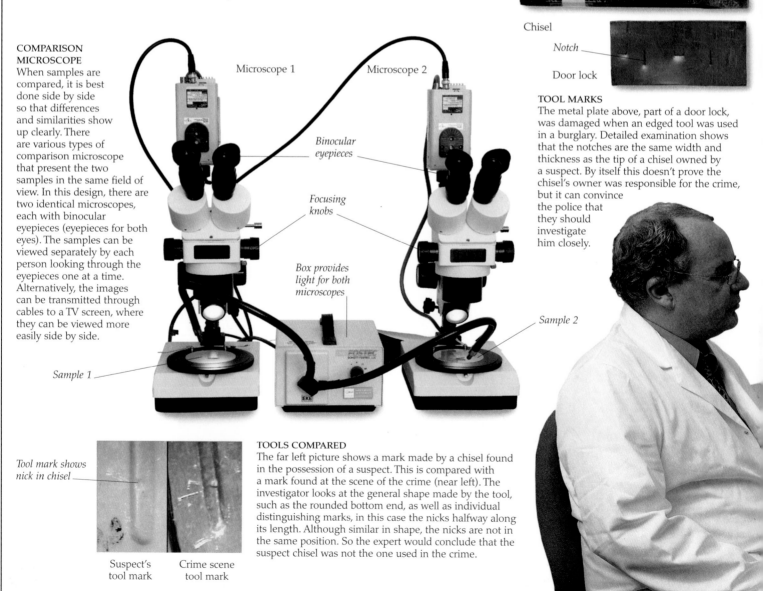

Microscope 1

Microscope 2

*Binocular eyepieces*

*Focusing knobs*

*Box provides light for both microscopes*

*Sample 1*

*Sample 2*

Chisel

*Notch*

Door lock

### TOOL MARKS
The metal plate above, part of a door lock, was damaged when an edged tool was used in a burglary. Detailed examination shows that the notches are the same width and thickness as the tip of a chisel owned by a suspect. By itself this doesn't prove the chisel's owner was responsible for the crime, but it can convince the police that they should investigate him closely.

*Tool mark shows nick in chisel*

Suspect's tool mark

Crime scene tool mark

### TOOLS COMPARED
The far left picture shows a mark made by a chisel found in the possession of a suspect. This is compared with a mark found at the scene of the crime (near left). The investigator looks at the general shape made by the tool, such as the rounded bottom end, as well as individual distinguishing marks, in this case the nicks halfway along its length. Although similar in shape, the nicks are not in the same position. So the expert would conclude that the suspect chisel was not the one used in the crime.

## THE SCANNING ELECTRON MICROSCOPE (SEM)

Forensic scientists use scanning electron microscopes (SEMs) to study trace evidence. Unlike microscopes that use light to provide a magnified image, SEMs rely on a stream of electrons. These tiny particles are electrically charged and when separated from their atoms, they form an electric current. In the SEM, the electron beam produces a highly magnified and very detailed image. Anything viewed under an SEM must be coated with metal so that the electric charge from the beam is conducted away. (If not, the charge builds up and interferes with the beam.) Here, a hair is stuck to a small metal disk, about $2/5$ in (1 cm) in diameter, which is coated with a layer of gold in order to be viewed under the SEM.

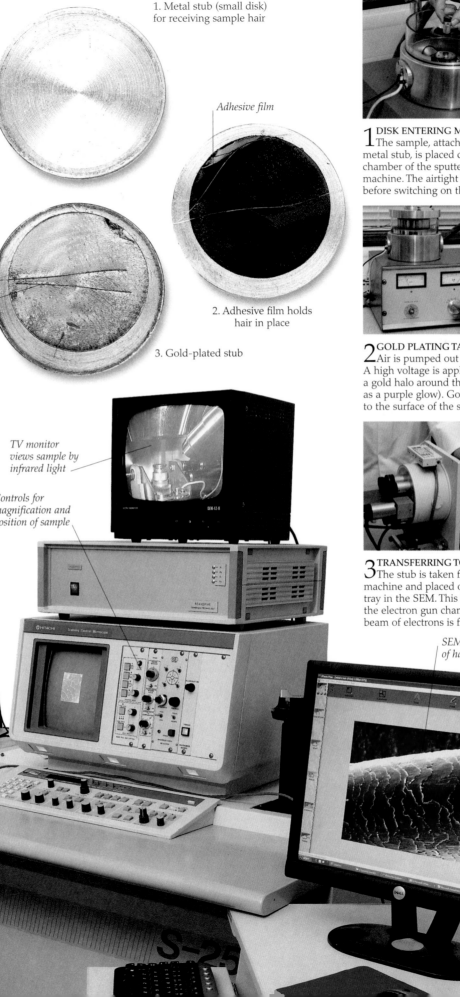

1. Metal stub (small disk) for receiving sample hair

*Adhesive film*

2. Adhesive film holds hair in place

*Hair visible through gold*

3. Gold-plated stub

### 4 FORMING A PICTURE
The beam of electrons is focused onto the sample by powerful electromagnets. The result appears on the computer monitor—a highly magnified, 3-D picture of the hair.

*Electron gun*

*Sample chamber*

*TV monitor views sample by infrared light*

*Controls for magnification and position of sample*

*SEM image of hair*

### 1 DISK ENTERING MACHINE
The sample, attached to the small metal stub, is placed carefully in the chamber of the sputtering (plating) machine. The airtight lid is closed before switching on the machine.

### 2 GOLD PLATING TAKING PLACE
Air is pumped out of the chamber. A high voltage is applied. This creates a gold halo around the sample (seen as a purple glow). Gold deposits stick to the surface of the sample.

### 3 TRANSFERRING TO SEM
The stub is taken from the coating machine and placed on a movable tray in the SEM. This is pushed into the electron gun chamber, and a beam of electrons is fired at it.

# Natural clues

FORENSICS EXPERTS KNOW that the air is always rich with almost invisible dust. Powerful microscopes reveal flakes of human and animal skin and tiny animals called dust mites in household dust. Outdoor dust in addition includes grains of sand, soil, and pollen. Dust may also contain human and animal hairs, and fibers from our clothes. According to Edmond Locard, the famous French forensics scientist, whenever two things or people touch, material from one is transferred to the other and vice versa. So at any crime scene—including on the victim and the guilty person—there are many "invisible" clues. Once removed to the laboratory, such clues can be looked at more closely and compared with known samples on databases. For example, it may be possible to identify the type and manufacturer of a carpet on the basis of a few fibers picked up at the scene, which might even solve the crime.

**SLIDE SHOW**
Specimens are mounted on slides—small glass plates—for viewing under the microscope. The scientist can tell if hair (top) is animal or human and whether fabric is synthetic (middle) or natural (bottom).

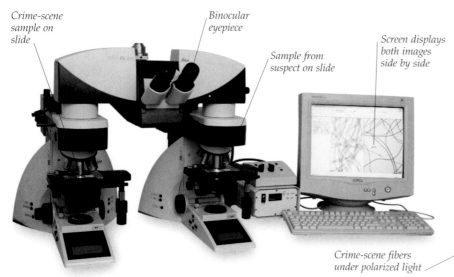

*Crime-scene sample on slide*

*Binocular eyepiece*

*Sample from suspect on slide*

*Screen displays both images side by side*

*Crime-scene fibers under polarized light*

**COMPARING FIBERS**
This advanced comparison microscope combines two microscopes. Two samples can be compared by observing through the binocular eyepiece, or on the computer screen. The central image (right) is a blown-up version of the screen. Two synthetic fiber samples are being compared: one is from the crime scene, the other from a suspect. The materials may be identified precisely by looking at the samples using polarized light. If the samples are found to be different, they provide no evidence that the suspect was at the crime scene. If they turn out to be the same, they provide some evidence, but not proof, that he or she was there.

**LOOKING AT HAIRS**
The color, type, and length of any hair found at the scene are all important clues but an SEM (scanning electron microscope) can show much more. The forensics expert looks for individual aspects of the hair that are not visible to the naked eye. The hair in the upper image is clearly damaged. This could be due to excessive use of hair-care products, which would immediately exclude some people. In the lower image, the blue specks are particles of dried shampoo, which may or may not be significant.

*Damaged hair shaft*

*Hair coated with shampoo particles*

**LOOKING AT POLLEN**
Under SEM, pollen spores are seen to have beautiful and intricate structures. In principle, the species of plant is clearly identifiable, but there are many thousands of plant species with which to compare the image so it is not always easy to find the right one. Each type of pollen is produced at definite times of year, so the presence of pollen in the clothing of a victim or suspect can give important clues about when and where they have been.

*Ragweed pollen*

*Multifaceted pollen grain*

*Sunflower pollen*

## GETTING IT TAPED

An investigator, wearing gloves, presses tape onto a wool sweater and peels it off, to collect loose fibers. This special adhesive tape is usually the best way of collecting fibers from clothing for investigation. The fibers may show where the wearer of the clothing has been, or who they have been in contact with. Sometimes an investigator will use tweezers to pick up single fibers, but tape is fast and picks up all the fibers. The tape plus fibers can be stored permanently in case investigators ever want to take a second look.

*Tape pulled across sweater*

*Wool and unidentified fibers seen sticking to tape*

### EDMOND LOCARD

Locard (1877–1966) was a leading French forensic scientist. During his lifetime his famous exchange principle—"every contact leaves a trace"—became more and more important, as scientific advances made it possible to detect even tinier traces at the scene of an incident. Among his many achievements was a huge textbook called *Treatise on Criminalistics*. (Criminalistics just means forensic science.)

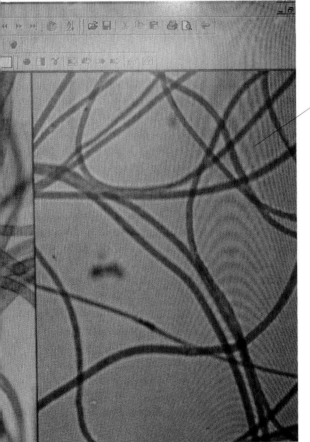

*Fibers from suspect under polarized light*

*Spectrometer's FTIR machine*

*Microscope's binocular eyepiece*

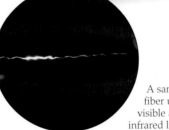

*A sample fiber under visible and infrared light*

### FINDING A FIBER'S IDENTITY

Comparison of different fibers or other materials is just one method of identifying their origin. Sometimes scientists have only one sample so comparison is not possible, but they still have to try and find out where the fiber has come from. The machine above is a spectrometer, which uses both visible light and invisible infrared light. (Infrared light has wavelengths longer than ordinary light.) A fiber is being examined (inset). Ordinary visible light is shining on the fiber, but an infrared beam is also focused on it. The FTIR (Fourier transform infrared spectroscopy) machine analyzes the reflected infrared light by a highly sophisticated technique. The machine's output is a graph, which can be compared to information stored in a huge database of common and not so common materials.

### SEEDS OF SUSPICION

Grass seeds solved the murder of Louise Almodovar in 1942. She was strangled on November 1 in Central Park, New York City. Her husband Anibal was held on suspicion. Witnesses testified that he had been dancing at a club that night, but it was only a few hundred yards from the murder spot. Grass seeds of a rare type were found in his pockets and pant cuffs. A botanist showed that in New York City they grew only in Central Park—at the spot where Louise had been killed. Anibal hurriedly produced a story about having walked in the park in September. The botanist pointed out that the grass produces its seeds in mid-October at the earliest. At this point, Almodovar broke down and confessed.

# A good impression

FOOTPRINTS, DENTS, AND SCRAPES are a treasure trove for forensic specialists. If there are footprints and tire tracks at a crime scene, the investigators make a record of them. This is done by taking photographs and possibly by making a cast—a solid copy in hard material. The patterns of shoe prints are cataloged and kept on a computerized database. An officer provides a description of a footprint, in terms of its size and the design of diamonds, curves, squares, and other lines that make up the pattern of the sole. With these details, full information about the brand, the date it went on the market, and a picture of the whole shoe can all be quickly found. The same thing can be done with prints of tires—then a list of all vehicles that use that make of tire can be called up. The marks that an intruder leaves when forcing windows or doors during a break-in are individual—often specific to a particular tool—and harder to track down.

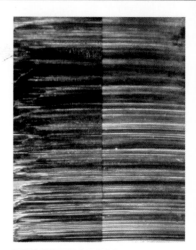

**BOLT-CUTTER MATCH**
Microscope photographs reveal the tool responsible for a break-in. Every cutting tool leaves its own "fingerprint" (pattern of marks). The left-hand picture above shows marks left on a chain-link that had been cut in a burglary. The right-hand picture shows marks made in a laboratory by a bolt-cutter found by the police. The pictures line up exactly, showing that the same blade made both cuts.

*Powerful flashlight*

*Additional light source*

*Ultraviolet light tube*

### LIFTING FOOTPRINTS
A footprint can be a faint mark consisting of dust. This investigator has a powerful flashlight with an additional lamp attached for extra power. Shining the light at an angle rather than directly often shows up faint footprints. Other kinds of light can show up different substances more strongly. Ultraviolet light, for example, makes some substances glow. The forensic scientist can make a permanent record of a dusty footprint that he can take away to examine more closely in a laboratory. He lays a sheet of foil-backed plastic film over the print, and touches a high-voltage probe to the film. Dust is attracted from the print to the film, forming an impression that can be fixed with a spray.

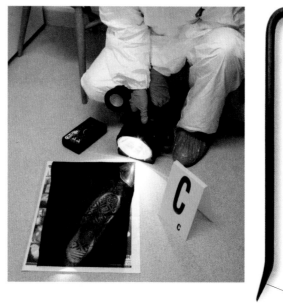

**BURGLAR'S TOOLS**
A crowbar and a chisel are two of a burglar's favorite tools. Fingerprints and unique marks on the blades of the instruments can give away their user's identity. Even the tiny fragments left after their use can provide clues; for example, they may have come from another crime scene if the criminal hasn't cleaned his tools well enough.

*Chisel*

*Crowbar*

### TIRE TRACKS
A track left by a vehicle tire, such as this one in soft ground could be a valuable clue, so a permanent record needs to be made. A photograph will do, but even better is a latex (rubber) cast made in the same way as a footprint cast (see p. 29). The image can be compared with a computerized database of tire treads to narrow down the type of vehicle and the date and place of its manufacture. In addition, there will be unique wear marks that may help identify the vehicle that made the track.

*Database tracks are compared with those from the scene*

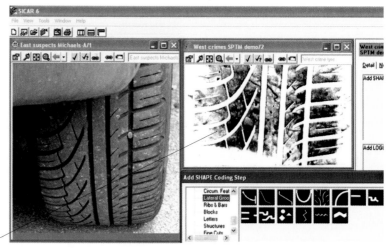

Rigid frame holds
print in place

Resin takes up
shape of print

## RECORDING A SHOE PRINT

A footprint found at a crime scene is a valuable, but only
temporary, piece of evidence. A cast must be made if
the print is to have any forensic value. The first stage in
making a cast is to pour resin (a liquid plastic) into the
depression of the print. A framework keeps the print in
position and retains the liquid. The liquid is left for a while
until it "sets" (hardens) into a flexible, rubberlike solid. The
pattern obtained is a negative of the shoe print—convex
where the print is concave and vice versa—so the next
step is to make a second cast from this one, which will
show the true shape of the print.

## THE SECOND CAST

The permanent record of the shoe print is made in the
laboratory with a hard material such as plaster of Paris.
Now the concave parts of the print are represented by
concave parts of the cast, convex parts by convex. The
pattern on the sole in this case is very clear, but also
very common. There are also many individual marks
made by wear and tear that will be unique to this shoe.

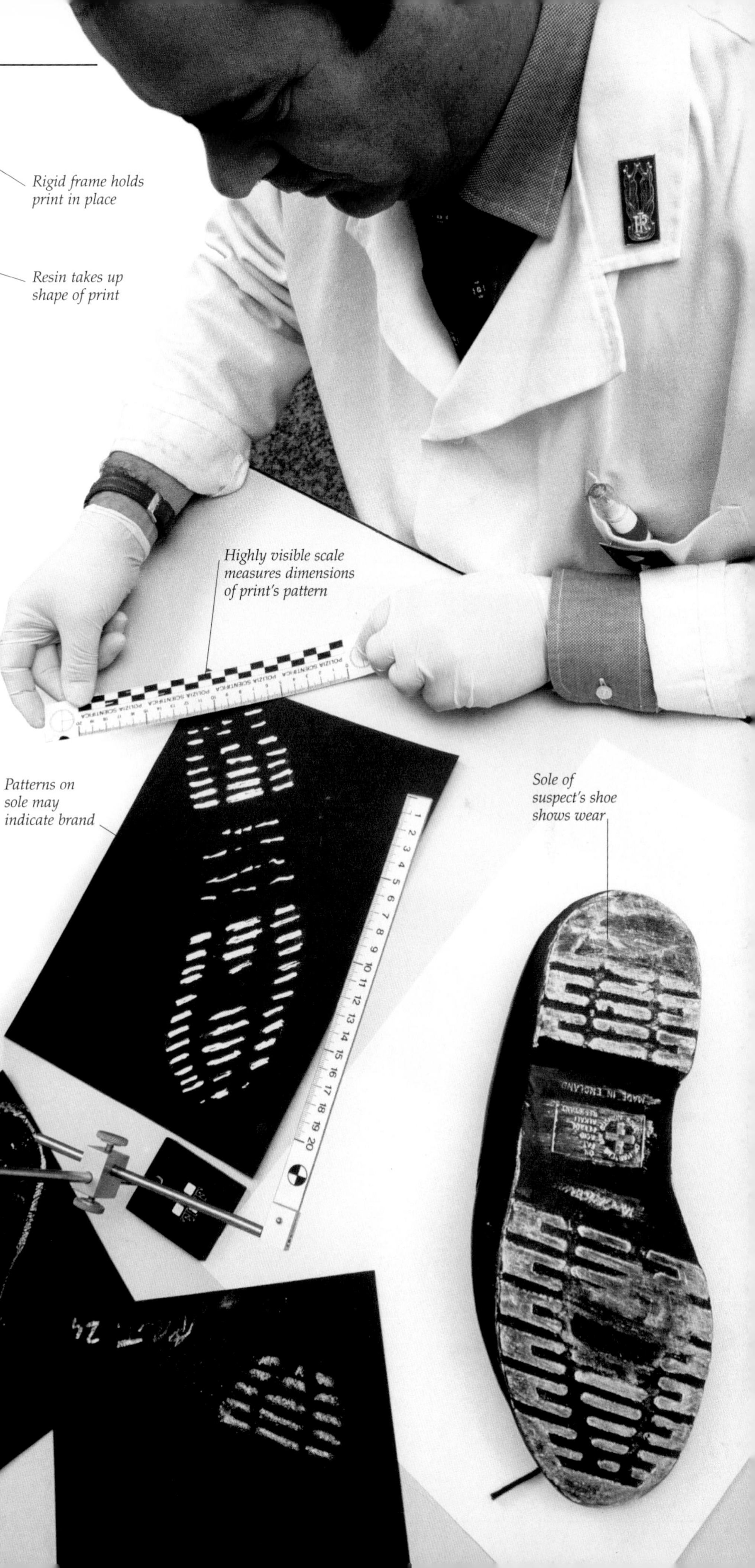

## MEASURING SHOE PRINTS

A forensic investigator measures the main
dimensions of the heel and sole of a suspect's
shoe. He uses a ruler to measure the shoe
print and its outline, as well as the
suspect's shoe. The measurements
can be used to file individual
records, in much the same
way as fingerprints are
stored in databases.

Highly visible scale
measures dimensions
of print's pattern

Patterns on
sole may
indicate brand

Sole of
suspect's shoe
shows wear

Outline of
shoe reveals
its size

# Guns and bullets

**OPERATION TRIDENT**
In 1998, London, England's Metropolitan Police set up a program, called "Operation Trident," which invited people to hand in guns and other weapons without fear of prosecution. The head of the initiative is shown with a cache of seized guns. Some had been used in violent crimes.

POLICE OFFICERS KNOW THE DEVASTATING HARM that firearms can cause. One of the first things to be done at any scene of crime where they have been used is to make safe any guns and ammunition that are present. The forensic investigation can then begin. The investigators record the positions of the weapons. They measure the damage caused by bullets to objects and human victims. They search for the bullets themselves—marks on them are like "fingerprints" of the weapons from which they were fired. The investigators carefully work out the positions from which the bullets were fired and the trajectories (paths) that they followed. They also search for tiny particles called firearm discharge residue (FDR) or gunshot residue (GSR), which are blasted out by a gunshot.

Twin triggers

Trigger guard

Stock

Rear sight

Foresight

Stock

Magazine clip

Trigger

Trigger guard

Safety catch

Rear sight

Hammer

Barrel

Slide

Foresight

Trigger guard

Grip

Trigger

13-round magazine within

Magazine release catch

**RIFLE**
A rifle is a long-barreled firearm that has spiral grooves called rifling running along the inside of its barrel. These make the bullet spin as it travels along the barrel, leaving characteristic marks on the bullet. The spin makes the bullet fly in a straighter path when it emerges. A rifle often has a magazine clip containing several cartridges (the bullet containers). The user steadies the rifle's stock against the shoulder when firing. This, the long barrel, the rifling, and (sometimes) a telescopic sight all make the rifle a very accurate firearm.

**PISTOL**
The Beretta 92FS is the pistol (handgun) that was adopted as the US military's official sidearm in 1985. Pistols like this are often called "automatics," but they are usually "semiautomatic," which means that a single pull of the trigger fires the bullet, ejects the used cartridge, and readies the next cartridge for firing. When the gun fires, the top part (slide) is driven back. A spring then forces it forward again to load the next cartridge into the chamber. A fully automatic weapon can fire repeated shots while the trigger is pressed once and held. Although intended for police and military use, such weapons have found their way into the hands of criminals.

## DEATH IN DALLAS

The 1963 assassination of President Kennedy showed the lethal capabilities of powerful guns in criminal hands. The president was riding in an open-topped car through Dallas, Texas. Ex-marine Lee Harvey Oswald fired three shots from a sixth-story warehouse window. One shot killed the president. To this day, conspiracy theories abound about who shot the president and why, but they are hard to prove so long after the event.

The motorcade just before the shooting

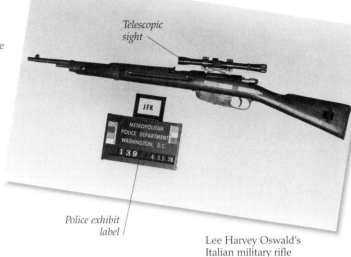

*Telescopic sight*

*Police exhibit label*

Lee Harvey Oswald's Italian military rifle

## SHOTGUN

A shotgun is a long-barreled firearm that fires many small pellets (called shot) enclosed in a shell, rather than a single bullet. Unlike a rifle, the inside of its barrel is smooth. Its aim is less accurate than a rifle's, but this is made up for by the wide dispersal of the shot, which makes it easy to hit a target at close range. Criminals often like to carry shotguns during robberies to terrify people. A sawed-off shotgun has a shortened barrel, which reduces its accuracy. This weapon is favored by criminals because it is easy to hide in a bag.

*Twin barrels for quick firing*

*Barrel*

*Plastic case*

*Metal head*

Pellets

## SHOTGUN SHELL

A normal shotgun shell contains many pellets, called shot, instead of a single bullet. These do not follow an accurate path, but spread out after leaving the barrel. The shotgun is good at hitting a close target, even when used by an inexperienced shooter. Shot can be of different sizes, described by a number—the larger the number, the smaller the shot.

## POWER OF THE GUN

Irrespective of shape or size, all guns produce an explosion that sends a bullet (or shot in shotguns) racing out of the barrel. In a rifle, the bullet is encased within a cartridge, together with gunpowder. A shotgun also holds cartridges, or shells, enclosing pieces of lead shot rather than a single bullet. With a pull of the trigger, the firing pin strikes and ignites the end of the cartridge, causing the gunpowder inside to explode. This forces the bullet or shot out of the gun with great speed.

## RIFLE CARTRIDGE

A rifle cartridge is longer and slimmer than a pistol cartridge. The case is filled with gunpowder and the pointed bullet is on top. It is made of lead, usually covered with a metal jacket to prevent buildup of lead in the rifle barrel.

## REPLICA BULLET

Although not designed to harm, these bullets can be made deadly by removing the plastic pellet inside and replacing it with a ball bearing. Replica guns are common in crime as they are easy to buy.

## MANIPULATED BULLET

A modified bullet—also known as a "dum-dum" bullet—is altered to do more damage when it hits a target. The bullet shown here has had the top of its metal jacket cut off, so that the jacket will spread when the bullet hits its target. If that target happens to be a human being, a larger, more damaging wound will be created, either at the point of impact or inside the body.

## PISTOL CARTRIDGE

A cartridge used in a pistol differs from a rifle cartridge. It is shorter and broader in relation to its length. The empty cartridge left behind after firing is immediately ejected from the gun by the force of the explosive power. This same force brings the next cartridge into the firing chamber. The cycle continues until all the ammunition is used up.

*Lead bullet*

*Gunpowder explodes and forces out bullet*

*Cartridge case*

*Primer ignites gunpowder*

Modified bullet

Standard bullet

Replica bullet

Rifle cartridge

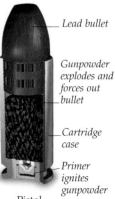

Pistol cartridge

# Firearms in the laboratory

THE STUDY OF GUN USE is called "ballistics." Internal ballistics is the study of the processes involved as the bullet is fired and travels down the barrel. Terminal ballistics is concerned with what happens when the bullet strikes the target. Chemistry is crucial, and analysis of firearm discharge residue (FDR) looks for key metals, including barium, antimony, and lead. The scanning electron microscope can form images of such particles, and can be used to analyze them chemically.

**BULLETS AND CARTRIDGES**
A rifle cartridge (bullet casing) is shown with two smaller pistol cartridges. The bullets have been separated from their cartridges and are shown at the top. The bullets are made of lead.

*Muffs, helmet, and eye shield protect shooter*

*Bracket holds gun steady at a specific angle*

**1 FIRING BULLET**
A forensic scientist fires a gun into a shooting tub filled with water. The investigator wears protective gear: earmuffs to protect his hearing, and a face mask in case of debris from the shot escaping in his direction. The bullet's trajectory is slowed down by the water inside.

**TEST FIRING**
In the forensic laboratory, a firearm of interest undergoes a test firing. The gun may have been found at the scene of crime, or elsewhere—perhaps in the possession of a suspect. After the test firing the marks made by the gun on the bullet and on the cartridge are examined. If they match those found on bullets or cartridges found at the scene, the weapon and its owner are linked to the crime. At national laboratories, new brands of gun are also tested, to find out what marks they leave on ammunition. A bullet picked up from a crime scene can then be checked against known bullet marks of new guns and the weapon identified.

**2 RETRIEVING THE BULLET**
From the water in the tub, the investigator drags out the fired bullets for examination. After microscopic examination, photographs of the markings produced by this particular weapon will be permanently stored on the computerized police database.

**SHOOTING TUB**
The path of a bullet fired from a particular gun can be tested in the shooting tub. A bullet is made of a dense metal—usually lead—so that, when used in a real situation, the drag of the air has less effect in slowing it. Water can stop a bullet in a surprisingly short distance.

*Shooting tub*

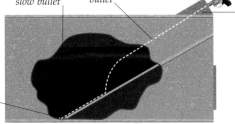

*Water to slow bullet*
*Path of bullet*
*Gun bracket*
*Bullet at rest*

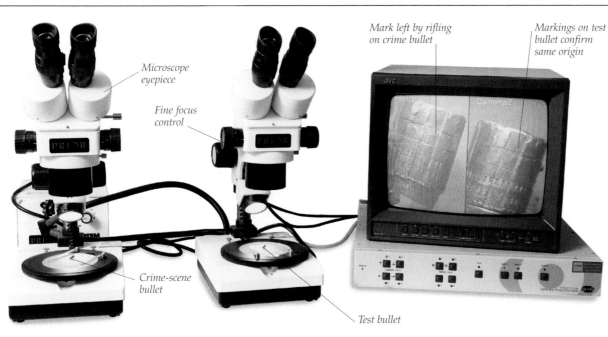

*Microscope eyepiece*

*Fine focus control*

*Mark left by rifling on crime bullet*

*Markings on test bullet confirm same origin*

*Crime-scene bullet*

*Test bullet*

## IMPACT DAMAGE
A bullet is grossly distorted (above right) when it hits anything solid—even comparatively soft wood. A test bullet fired into a water tub (above left) is much less seriously damaged. Even so, the two can be compared for striations (grooves) and rifling on the sides of the bullet behind the deformed head. Even a deformed bullet indicates which types of gun could have fired it, and the distance from which it was fired.

## SIGNATURE OF A GUN
A bullet from a crime scene is placed under a comparison microscope together with a bullet fired in the laboratory from a suspect weapon, in order to compare them at high magnification. The forensic investigator will be looking for several features in the comparison. Marks are left on the rear end of the cartridge when it is forced into the chamber on loading. Marks are also left by the hammer or firing-pin when it is fired. The rifling from the barrel leaves characteristic grooves running the length of the bullet. The best that such examination can achieve is to show a link between a gun and a crime. More evidence—for example, the discovery of a matching type of gunshot residue or a DNA link—is necessary to say conclusively that a particular person fired a particular shot.

## RETRIEVING A CARTRIDGE

A forensics officer places a used cartridge into an evidence bag at the scene of crime, after marking and photographing its position. Cartridges are automatically ejected from most types of firearm, and a criminal rarely has time to grab them before fleeing, so they are a frequent source of information.

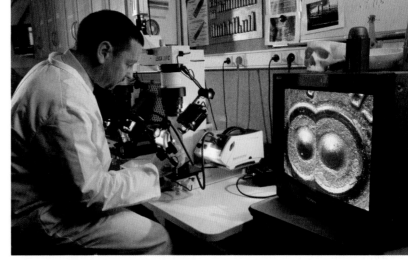

## COMPARING CARTRIDGE CASES
Two cartridges, one from the crime scene and one from a test firing in the laboratory, are being studied under a comparison microscope. Visible here are the rims of the cartridges, and the central percussion caps, which are struck by the weapon's firing pin. Both these areas at the rear of the cartridge, being in contact with parts of the weapon, will carry markings that are unique to that weapon. Under high magnification, similarities and differences between these markings are visible and can help the investigator decide whether there is a connection between the two cartridge cases.

## CONDEMNED BY BALLISTICS

The trial of Nicola Sacco and Bartolomeo Vanzetti was a sensation. In 1920, two payroll guards were shot and $16,000 was stolen in Braintree, Massachusetts. Sacco and Vanzetti were tried for the crime. They were political activists and many allies protested their innocence. The evidence against them was weak, but a firearms expert showed that the markings on a test bullet fired from Sacco's revolver matched those of one of the fatal bullets. The men were executed in August 1927.

Vanzetti

Sacco

## DEADLY PATH
A policeman is using a rod to reconstruct the path followed by a bullet that struck this car. Laser beams or strings are sometimes used instead. If a bullet hole is deep enough, the police may slide a probe into it to show the direction of entry. Tracing trajectories in this way is especially important if more than one person was using a gun at the scene.

*Probable position of gun*

*Rod links bullet hole with gun's position*

# At the scene of the crime

A CRIME INVESTIGATION doesn't always begin with a crime scene or a body: it may be sparked by a missing-person's report. The police have to choose whether to launch a search right away, at the risk of finding that the person has simply gone away without telling anyone. The alternative is to wait until it is certain that something is wrong, when the trail may have gone cold and many clues may have been lost. If a person is found dead at a scene, whether following a search or not, the first question is who are they; the second is whether the death is due to foul play. Even a death arising in the course of a crime is not necessarily a murder. All the clues have to be collected that might help a court decide whether the death was due to accident, negligence, recklessness—or murder.

**SNIFFING IT OUT**
Sniffer dogs are shown here searching the scene after an unsuccessful bomb attack at Glasgow Airport in Scotland. Dogs are also used to find drugs, and missing people—dead or alive. Some dogs are specially trained to scent a dead body, even if buried—springer spaniels (left) are one breed that make good "cadaver dogs," as they are called.

**EYE IN THE SKY**
A police helicopter crew liaises with police and volunteer searchers on the ground before continuing its flight in quest of a missing person. Using a helicopter is a costly method of search but it can cover a wide area and access areas that would prove difficult for land vehicles. That is why it is the equipment of choice in incidents involving the sea, lakes, mountains, moors, deserts, and other inhospitable terrain. It can also carry infrared heat detectors and other sophisticated devices capable of detecting a living or dead human body from the air.

*Cockpit provides 180° vision*

## WHO'S WHO

In the aftermath of a shooting outside a railroad station, the search to identify the victim begins. A clean-suited officer carries a stack of yellow position cards ready to be placed by evidence, which will be photographed and put into bags for safekeeping. Documents and other personal effects found on or near the body are included in this catalog since they will provide vital information to help identify the body. Friends or relatives may come forward with information, which may add to the picture. In this case, the victim who was shot was simply an innocent bystander who had intervened when criminals attacked two security guards.

### THE BODY FARM

Dr. William Bass looks at a body at the Body Farm—a research center in the US that studies how bodies decompose. Bodies are buried in different types of soil, or left out in the open or in the trunks of cars. Studying the way in which the bodies decompose can help pinpoint time of death. Many people donate their bodies to the Body Farm.

### A TRIPLE KILLER

In December 1993, "Big Mike" Rubenstein reported finding three of his relatives—a man, woman, and child—dead in their mountain cabin. He had visited twice in November and found the cabin empty, he said. Body Farm scientists used their knowledge of how bodies decay to determine that the victims had died in mid-November—so their corpses must already have been there when Rubenstein said the cabin was empty. He was eventually convicted of the three murders.

### GOING DEEP

A diver searches a shallow stream in a hunt for a missing woman. Some of her possessions were found in the water, near where the diver was looking. Divers usually work in extremely poor visibility. However, they are now increasingly aided by sonar equipment, using high-frequency sound waves to generate an image of objects on the bottom. When this indicates objects of potential interest, divers go underwater to investigate them.

### RADAR DOWN TO EARTH

A searcher steers a GPR (ground-penetrating radar) unit. GPR can be used when a body or other evidence is suspected to be buried in a well-defined area. The unit sends out radar (high-frequency radio) waves. These are reflected more strongly by some objects beneath the ground than by others. The image has to be interpreted by an expert and rarely shows definitely that a body is buried. However, what it can do is give a good indication that something unusual is present and with this knowledge experts can decide if it is worth conducting a more thorough search.

*Police officer gives instructions to volunteers*

*Underground details relayed to monitor*

*Net encloses blowfly
incubator, used to study
lifecycle of insect*

# A bug's life

**W**ITHIN MINUTES OF A PERSON DYING, the flies arrive. They are guided by substances released by decomposing bodies—such as "cadaverine" (a cadaver is a corpse) or "putrescine" (putrescence is decomposition). The flies are the first of many types of insects to come and set up house on the corpse. Some insects eat the flesh themselves, but most come to lay eggs so that their developing young have a ready supply of food. The young that emerge from eggs are called larvae, and are very different in form from the adult. Other insect species come in waves, the later arrivals feeding on the larvae of the earlier ones. The young grow at a fairly definite rate for each species. The forensic entomologist (someone who studies insects) can often figure out the time of death from a study of the insects and larvae on a corpse.

**MITE**
Mites arrive on a dead body soon after flies. They often eat eggs and maggots of other insects, misleading forensic scientists.

**MOVING IN**
The different species of insect that inhabit a corpse, and the order in which they arrive at their "cafeteria," can provide many clues for the forensic entomologist. Insects colonize a body in a definite pattern: blowflies arrive first; rove beetles come at 4–7 days after death, followed closely by wasps; at 8–18 days, ants, cockroaches, and other beetle species are present; clothes moths are among the final visitors, coming when most of the fleshy parts of the body have already been eaten. As a very general rule, if the only signs of habitation are eggs, death has probably occurred in the past 24 hours. At the other extreme, hatched adults at the scene suggest death happened around two to three weeks earlier.

**SPRINGTAIL BEETLE**
Springtails are among the later insects to arrive at a corpse—they can indicate the person died some time ago.

**WASP**
Wasps do not usually feed on corpses, but on the insects that have arrived earlier. They may also lay their eggs in the maggots on the body.

*Water for
consistent humidity*

*Blowfly pupae*

**MAGGOT FARM**
This net houses a family of blowfly pupae growing on rotting meat in a forensic science laboratory. The scientists study their rate of growth, the stages they go through, the effects of light and temperature, and the effects on insect development of drugs or alcohol in the meat—this imitates the effects of these substances in dead bodies. All this information is valuable to forensic scientists trying to figure out the time and place of a suspicious death. Investigators carry out a similar process of growing eggs, maggots, or pupae from the scene. Since larvae of different species and different ages can look similar, they have to be grown to maturity to identify what insects are present, and their stage of development.

**CLOTHES MOTH**
In the final stages of decomposition, the larvae of clothes moths may feed on the corpse's hair.

**ANTS**
Although not partial to human flesh, ants are often found on and around a dead body. They are interested in feasting on the larvae and maggots of some of the other insects that are feeding from the corpse.

## 4 ADULT

Two to three weeks after the blowfly's eggs were first laid, the fully formed adult flies emerge from the pupae. They have all the characteristics of flies, including six legs, a single pair of wings, and eyes that are huge relative to the size of their bodies. The adults do not feed on flesh—only the maggots do this, in order to prepare for adulthood. The time taken for the adult to emerge is strongly dependent on temperature—the warmer the surroundings, the faster the development.

*24 hours*

## 1 EGGS

Each adult female blowfly that arrives at the corpse will lay about 250 eggs in the ears, nose, other openings, wounds, or folds in clothing—wherever it is warm and moist. The eggs are incredibly small, each one measuring about $1/12$ in (2 mm) in length. Through the translucent outer layers of the eggs, a faint mass—which is, in fact, the future larva—becomes visible. It takes only about 24 hours for the eggs to develop into the next stage of the cycle.

*24 hours*

## LIFE CYCLE OF THE BLOWFLY

Blowflies are a family of insects that includes many species. Some of these are the familiar metallic-looking bluebottles. All blowflies lay their eggs on the flesh of decomposing bodies, and also on open wounds. The first blowflies to arrive at a fresh corpse typically show up within minutes. For this reason, the eggs, larvae, pupae, and adult forms of the fly found on a corpse are one of the best guides to the time since death. A forensic investigator will collect all the insect life he or she can see on or near the corpse and will grow them to maturity in the laboratory to identify them.

*7 days*

*7–14 days (three larval stages occur)*

## 3 PUPA

The pupa is the stage of development during which the blowfly turns from a shapeless maggot into the adult fly. The maggot first develops a hard casing, or puparium. The transformation from larva to adult takes place hidden inside this apparently lifeless casing. The pupa cannot move or feed, and lives off food stored in its body. It spends as long as a week in this state. Then the newly developed fly forces its way out.

## 2 MAGGOTS

Blowfly eggs develop into maggots. A maggot is an insect larva that is blind and legless, but able to move by wriggling, and able to feed. Blowfly maggots in a corpse molt, or lose their skins, twice, to go through three stages, each bigger than the previous one. If the maggots cluster into masses, they generate heat and attract other insects that feed on them. The last maggot stage ends one to two weeks after the eggs were laid.

## MAGGOTS GIVE THE GAME AWAY

The charred remains of a man were found in a burned-out car 18 days after he'd been reported missing. The corpse was studied by the forensic entomologists at the Body Farm of the University of Tennessee. There were live maggots on his body, and from their size and weight, they were judged to be 2 days old. Did that mean the man had been dead for only 2 days? In his brain, there were also dead maggots. These had developed for about 14 to 16 days before they had been cooked in the fire. The investigators concluded that the man had been killed soon after his disappearance. Two weeks after his murder, the criminal had tried to disguise the cause of death by burning the car with the body in it. Insects returned to colonize the cooled body.

*A burned-out car can initially disguise the cause of death*

# Cause of death

A POSTMORTEM (after-death) examination, or autopsy, begins with an external assessment of the state of the body. This is conducted by a scientist called a forensic pathologist, who looks for signs of injury. With stab or bullet wounds, it is necessary to study the angle of impact and the depth of penetration. Next, the pathologist cuts open the body to check the internal organs for further clues as to why the person died. The organs are removed and pieces of tissue are cut from them to be sent for laboratory analysis. This may reveal that death was caused by, say, a lack of oxygen due to carbon monoxide poisoning or suffocation. Finally, the organs are replaced and the body is sewn up so that it can be buried or cremated.

## AUTOPSY ROOM
A body that has to be examined is brought from the mortuary (see p. 39) to an autopsy room—an operating room for the dead. Here a pathologist pieces together the facts behind a suspicious death. The body is placed on a specially designed stainless-steel table. After the body has been cleaned, the pathologist gets to work. Hygiene in the autopsy room is of utmost importance, both to protect the pathologist's health and to ensure that the evidence is not contaminated. Any organs removed are weighed, since an abnormal organ weight may indicate the cause of death.

*Refrigerated cabinet for storing body parts*

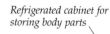

*Raised lip prevents liquids from spilling on to floor*

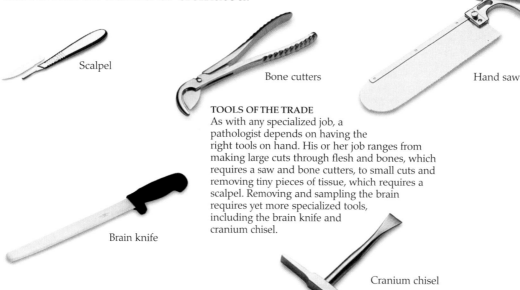

Scalpel

Bone cutters

Hand saw

Brain knife

Cranium chisel

## TOOLS OF THE TRADE
As with any specialized job, a pathologist depends on having the right tools on hand. His or her job ranges from making large cuts through flesh and bones, which requires a saw and bone cutters, to small cuts and removing tiny pieces of tissue, which requires a scalpel. Removing and sampling the brain requires yet more specialized tools, including the brain knife and cranium chisel.

## AUTOPSY PROCEDURE
If the initial examination of the body indicates suspicious circumstances, the pathologist will open up the body. He or she uses special surgical saws to cut through bone, and surgical tools to cut out and into each organ. The procedure follows a set sequence. First to be pulled out are the esophagus and stomach. (The esophagus is the tube that leads from the mouth to the stomach.) Then out come the heart and lungs, followed by the brain. Finally, the liver and kidneys are removed.

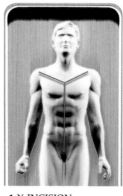

**1 Y-INCISION**
The first cut (or "incision") is Y-shaped—across the chest and down the body.

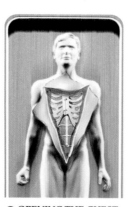

**2 OPENING THE CHEST**
The pathologist peels back the flesh of the chest to reveal the rib cage and the soft organs.

**3 ACCESS TO ORGANS**
The front ribs are removed using a saw. The internal organs can now be removed.

## EXAMINING THE BRAIN
If the brain needs to be examined, the top of the skull is removed and the brain is first studied in position. Then its connection to the spinal cord is cut and the brain is removed and weighed. The organ can be kept in formalin, a preserving fluid, until it is returned to the skull for burial.

*Scales for
weighing organs*

*Chalk board for recording
weights of organs*

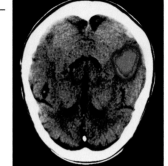

## DEATH IN THE BRAIN

A major cause of death in violent crimes is a hemorrhage (bleeding) inside the skull, resulting from a blow to the head. If there are no outward signs of injury, the cause of death may not be apparent, so pathologists must open the skull to look for evidence. Brain scans can reveal hemorrhages without opening the skull, but they are usually only performed on living people. This scan shows bleeding (red area) in a 66-year-old woman. It did not prove fatal.

## CUT TO THE BONE

Stab wounds can be so severe that they penetrate the soft tissues and go deep enough to damage the victim's bones, leaving clear marks. Just as burglary tools can be identified by the marks they leave at the crime scene (see pp. 24 and 28), pathologists can sometimes link a particular weapon to the stabbing, because imperfections in the blade match the marks it left on the bones.

*Groove made by
knife blade*

Fragment of
thigh bone

## TISSUE ANALYSIS

After an autopsy, scientists in a laboratory analyze tissue samples removed from the various organs to see what information they can yield. Blood is tested for its group, and to see what diseases the person might have had. Testing hair can reveal whether and when the person had taken drugs. However, the most important tissue test is DNA typing (see pp. 22–23), which can be performed on a wide range of body tissues and fluids.

*Autopsy table slopes
toward drain at far end*

*Water to clean body and wash
away fluids released by autopsy*

## AUTOPSY RECORD

As part of the general external examination of a body before it is cut open, the pathologist will usually draw a diagram showing all notable features—birthmarks, moles, tattoos, and so on, as well as any wounds, bruises, or other markings that may possibly be linked to the person's death. Increasingly, photography is also being used to record body marks, but photos still need to be interpreted and annotated by the pathologist. Often a pathologist will tape an audio commentary during the examination. The goal of all this is to ensure that a complete record is made of all the information at the time of the examination, so that later anaylsis does not have to rely on half-remembered facts.

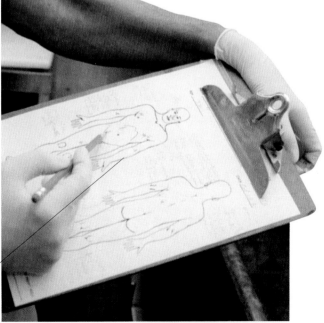

*Notable features
marked on standard
autopsy diagram*

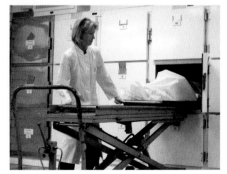

## THE MORTUARY

Dead bodies are kept in a storage room called a mortuary, or morgue. Each body is kept in a body bag in a separate large drawer. If an autopsy is needed, or if the person has not yet been identified, the body is kept chilled so that it does not decompose and its condition remains much the same as at the time of death. After an autopsy, a body is returned to its drawer in the mortuary until burial or cremation.

# Toxic world

IF DRUG USE OR POISONING is suspected in a crime, samples from an autopsy or crime scene may be sent to toxicologists, who test them for toxins. A toxin is any substance that is harmful, or poisonous, to the human body. The drugs we take for our health are medicines. Drugs taken for pleasure range from the mild stimulant caffeine (found in coffee, tea, and cola drinks), through alcohol and nicotine (the active ingredient in tobacco), to more powerful and harmful illegal drugs such as cannabis, cocaine, and heroin. Any drug can be toxic, even fatal, if taken in excess or used for the wrong purposes. In addition to looking for toxins in bodies, forensic scientists also investigate toxic hazards produced by our way of life. Industrial wastes are often toxic, and new and poorly tested materials can pose health risks.

**WARNING—POISON!**
Emblazoned on pirate flags long ago to instill fear in their enemies, the skull and crossbones symbol is still used today to warn of deadly danger. Seen on a chemical bottle, or on the door of a cabinet or room, the skull and crossbones means that there is poison—a toxic substance—inside. The implications of this traditional and universal symbol are understood by the public around the world.

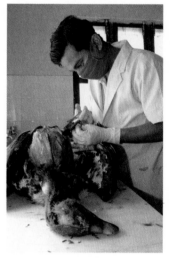

**ENVIRONMENTAL CRIME?**
Not all crime victims are human. A scientist studies the corpse of an Indian white-backed vulture that was allegedly killed by an environmental toxin. The cause might have been natural, or it might have been criminal activity—farmers deliberately setting out poison to protect their animals from predators, or a factory negligently releasing a harmful waste product. In fact, this vulture and many others seem to have been killed by feeding on the carcasses of cows that had been given diclofenac, a veterinary drug.

**ANTHRAX ATTACK**
On September 11, 2001, hijacked airliners destroyed the twin skyscrapers of the World Trade Center in New York City and damaged the Pentagon military headquarters in Washington, D.C. Nearly 3,000 people were killed. One week later, another terrorist attack against the United States began. Five letters containing spores of the deadly disease anthrax were sent to news companies and two US senators. Five people died and 17 others were infected. Millions of dollars were spent trying to locate the source, decontaminate dozens of office buildings, and screen mail to prevent future anthrax attacks. The spores must have been prepared in a laboratory—and the type involved was first prepared at a US research laboratory in the 1980s—but the source was never identified and no arrests were made.

A forensic scientist checks a suspect package

One of the letters
containing anthrax

**A CLASSIC MURDERER**
When the remains of the missing Cora Crippen, wife of Englishman Dr. Hawley Harvey Crippen, were found buried in his basement he was already on board a ship bound for Canada with his lover. The ship's captain reported by radio that he'd recognized the fugitives, even though both were well disguised. A Scotland Yard officer boarded a faster ship and was waiting for them when they arrived in Canada. Crippen was found guilty of poisoning his wife and was hanged in November 1910.

## TESTING FOR TOXINS

An important part of the forensic scientist's job is to identify toxins in samples taken from a crime scene or a victim's body. Even a tiny amount of some toxins can be deadly. One of the most sensitive instruments for analyzing small quantities of a substance is the mass spectrometer. It breaks up a sample into tiny molecules (groups of atoms). Molecules of different substances have different masses. By separating the molecules according to their mass, the spectrometer tells the scientist which substances the sample contains.

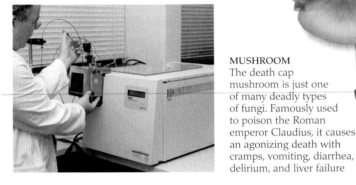

### 1 INJECTING THE SAMPLE
A small amount of the sample is inserted into the mass spectrometer. Electron beams bombard the sample, knocking electrons out of the molecules. This turns the molecules into electrically charged particles called ions.

### 2 PINBALL SCIENCE
The mass spectrometer then plays "pinball" with the ions. A strong electric field fires the ions in a beam up the machine (from the bottom left-hand corner), and a magnetic field bends the beam around the curved track. Ions of different substances have different masses, so they follow different paths and separate out by the time they reach the detector (bottom right). The result is a graph showing if any toxins are present.

## POISONS

Historically, poisons were a firm favorite with murderers, since it was often possible to make it look as if the victim had died naturally. With today's sophisticated toxicology, few criminals could hope to get away with murder using any of the three poisons below. But accidental poisonings occur and forensic scientists may be called in to investigate.

### MUSHROOM
The death cap mushroom is just one of many deadly types of fungi. Famously used to poison the Roman emperor Claudius, it causes an agonizing death with cramps, vomiting, diarrhea, delirium, and liver failure

### STRYCHNINE
The toxic leaves of strychnine cause a very unpleasant, slow death. Violent convulsions lasting some time eventually cause exhaustion and lung paralysis, which leads to suffocation.

### ANTIMONY
This metal was once ground up and used in powdered form as a poison. It has a distinctive metal taste that is hard to disguise, so it would be given in small doses over a long period. Antimony ultimately causes death by heart failure.

## ILLEGAL DRUGS

Some drugs, such as marijuana, heroin, amphetamines, and cocaine, are so detrimental to health that their use is prohibited by law. In some countries alcohol is also illegal. If taken in large enough quantities, or in a "cocktail" with other drugs, these drugs can produce life-threatening symptons. If there are no signs of injury in a dead person, a toxicologist may test for evidence of drugs in the blood.

### CANNABIS
Also known as marijuana, this is the most commonly used illegal drug. Strong concentrations of the drug have been known to cause abnormal behavior, so victims and suspects in apparently motiveless crimes are often tested for cannabis.

## KILLED BY RICIN

Walking in London one day in 1978, Georgi Markov felt a jab in the back of his leg. He turned to see a man behind picking up a fallen umbrella and apologizing to him. The man jumped into a taxi and Markov thought no more of it. Three days later, Markov was dead. The umbrella was a weapon that had injected him with a tiny metal pellet containing the deadly poison ricin. Markov was a political dissident who protested about conditions in his home country of Bulgaria, and he was almost certainly assassinated by a Bulgarian agent.

*Drilled hole to hold ricin*

Actual size of pellet

### HEROIN
Extracted from the opium poppy plant, heroin is a highly addictive drug and is commonly abused. Accidental overdose often causes death in addicts. Toxicologists can determine from a blood test whether heroin was responsible for the death.

# The bones of the matter

**BARE BONES**
The remains of a human being, reduced to mere bones after burial, are laid out on a forensic scientist's table. The investigator will almost certainly be able to tell the sex of the person, and also the height and age when he or she died. The ethnic group and state of health, and possibly even the cause of death, may also be revealed.

ONE STRAND OF INVESTIGATION is called forensic anthropology (the study of humankind for evidence). It is a branch of physical anthropology, which looks at how the human body varies among different peoples around the globe. Forensic anthropologists deal mainly with the skeleton—the part of a body that lasts longest when it's buried. People's skeletons change throughout their lives, which is why the size of the body in relation to the size of the head is greater in an adult than in a child. Skeletons also differ according to sex. The pelvis (consisting of the hip bones and a couple of smaller bones) is wider in a woman to allow for childbirth. In addition, skeletons vary around the world according to their ethnic origin. For example, there are significant differences between the skull shapes of Europeans, Africans, and East Asians. Forensic anthropologists sift through all this information to construct an accurate picture of the person whose bones they are investigating.

**ETHNIC COMPARISON**
The part of the skeleton that yields most information is the skull. To find a person's likely ethnic origin an anthropologist examines the depth (front to back) and breadth (side to side) of the skull. Other clues come from the cheekbones, eye sockets, and angle of the face, as well as the nose bridge and nasal opening. Teeth, too, are useful indicators of ethnic identity. The result is never conclusive, since there are wide variations within each ethnic population.

**EUROPEAN SKULL**
Skulls of Europeans are not as deep as those of Africans, nor as broad as those of East Asians. The face is relatively flat, since neither the cheekbones nor the jaw project.

*Less deep than African skull*

**AFRICAN SKULL**
Skulls of people from sub-Saharan Africa, or whose ancestors are from there, are deeper than those of Europeans. The cheekbones are lower, while the eye-sockets are wider, with more space between them.

*Wide space between eyes*

**EAST ASIAN SKULL**
Skulls of people from East Asia are long, and broad in relation to their depth, with rounded eye sockets. The incisors (the front cutting" teeth) are shovel-shaped.

*Broad forehead*

**MASS GRAVES**
United Nations forensic scientists dig at a communal grave in the Kosovo region of Serbia. In the late 1990s, civil war raged between the Serbian government and Kosovo, whose people are mostly of Albanian descent. Accusations of the mass murder of civilians were given credibility when communal graves were discovered. The investigators try to reunite the bodies' scattered bones to find out who the victims were (or at least which ethnic group they came from) and how they died.

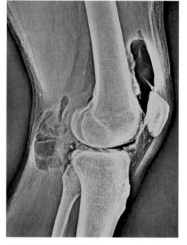

**ARTHRITIC KNEE**
This X-ray of a knee joint shows little space between the bones, which is a sign of osteoarthritis. In this disease, the cartilage (elastic connecting tissue) in knees, hips, and other joints wears away, so bones rub together and get damaged. After death, this person might be identifiable from medical records describing their condition.

*Reconstruction of head in clay*

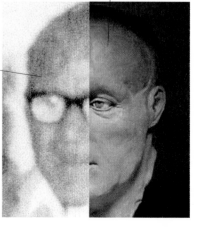

*Photo of missing man*

**FROM THE ASHES**
On November 18, 1987, a fire swept through King's Cross subway station in London, England. The identities of 30 people who died were pieced together over the days that followed. But one of the dead remained unidentified. Forensic sculptors reconstructed what they thought he had looked like from his fire-damaged skull (right). The victim was a short man who had undergone brain surgery. It was 15 years before the family of a homeless man, Alexander Fallon, 72 years old at the time of the fire, connected him with the event and matched his photo to the restoration.

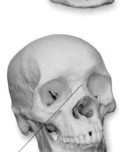

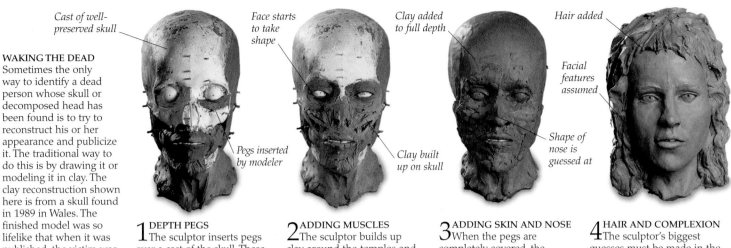

*Cast of well-preserved skull*

*Face starts to take shape*

*Clay added to full depth*

*Hair added*

*Facial features assumed*

*Pegs inserted by modeler*

*Clay built up on skull*

*Shape of nose is guessed at*

## WAKING THE DEAD
Sometimes the only way to identify a dead person whose skull or decomposed head has been found is to try to reconstruct his or her appearance and publicize it. The traditional way to do this is by drawing it or modeling it in clay. The clay reconstruction shown here is from a skull found in 1989 in Wales. The finished model was so lifelike that when it was published, the victim was immediately identified by her social worker.

**1 DEPTH PEGS**
The sculptor inserts pegs over a cast of the skull. These show the typical depth of facial flesh and muscle on a person of the same sex and age.

**2 ADDING MUSCLES**
The sculptor builds up clay around the temples and jaw, representing the muscles and underlying flesh in those areas.

**3 ADDING SKIN AND NOSE**
When the pegs are completely covered, the sculptor smoothes clay (representing the skin) over the whole skull.

**4 HAIR AND COMPLEXION**
The sculptor's biggest guesses must be made in the final stages, when he adds the hair, colors the skin, and hints at an expression.

## COMPUTER MODELING
Facial reconstruction is increasingly being done by computer, using data from CT (computer tomography) scans of living people. CT is a special type of X-ray scanning that detects soft tissue as well as bone—conventional X-rays reveal only bone. A CT scan of a head shows not only the skull shape, but also the depth of the overlying flesh. To "flesh out" the skull of an unknown person, the computer wraps a CT scan around a digital model of the skull, then stretches and squashes it to fit. Once facial details such as skin, eye color, and hair have been added, the reconstruction is ready to send out to police forces and the media.

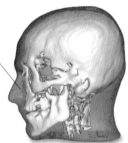

*The facial tissue fits neatly over the skull shape*

**4 ADDED EXTRAS**
After the CT skull is warped and merged with the model, the computer adds the CT scan's flesh and muscle tissues (blue).

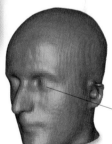

*Head resembles a clay model*

**5 SOLID RESULT**
The computer generates a 3-D, 360° view, but it's not yet lifelike. Details of eyes and hair are added—sometimes from other evidence, sometimes by guesswork.

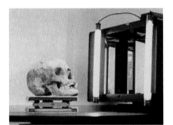

**1 SCANNING A SKULL**
A skull of an unidentified person rotates in front of a scanner in the University of Sheffield, England. A laser beam scans it, sending numerical information about its shape and size to a computer's memory. Now comes the challenge of reconstructing

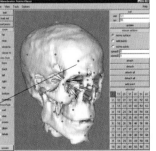

*Computer uses the landmarks as reference points when attaching the CT scan*

**2 PREPARING A MODEL**
The scanned skull is displayed on the computer screen as a digital model. The computer marks approximately the points where a CT scan will be fitted to the skull. These "landmark" points need to be positioned precisely. This fine-tuning is done by a human operator.

**3 BEST FIT**
A CT scan of a suitable skull is chosen from the computer's database, according to the forensic anthropologist's judgment of the sex, age, and race of the unkown person. The CT scan (red) is then superimposed on the model (blue) to show where they match and where the CT scan must be "warped" (distorted) to fit.

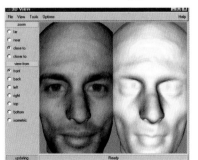

**6 BACK FROM THE DEAD**
To add authentic skin detail, a photo of a living face is wrapped around the model. Lastly, to make the face look realistic the computer adds highlights and shadows.

# Spitting image

WHEN A CRIME HAS BEEN COMMITTED, getting a good picture of a suspect or a victim is vital. A likeness can be circulated to police officers and published in the press and on TV, recruiting millions of members of the public in a bid to find a criminal or identify someone whose remains have been found. The first source police go to is often any CCTV cameras in the area of an incident. CCTV (closed-circuit television) is non-broadcast TV, such as security cameras in stores and public places. If no pictures are available, or none is of sufficiently good quality, a picture of the person's face will be made from witness descriptions. People tend to be poor at describing faces in words, but they are usually good at judging whether a picture, on screen or paper, is a close resemblance to a face they have seen. The police method of producing a likeness from a witness consists of building up a picture of the face from different components, while the witness says whether it's getting more or less like the person they saw. Originally this was done by drawing a picture freehand under the witness's direction. Then ready-made drawings of facial features were used, and later on photographs. Today's computers can build up images with an even higher degree of accuracy from witness descriptions.

**FACES IN A BOX**
A photographic identification kit was a great advance in getting descriptions of suspects from eyewitnesses. Facial features were broken down into a fixed number of types and then put on to photographic cards. The technique was invented by a photographer, Jacques Penry, who called his system "Photo-Fit." It was capable of creating 15 billion different faces. This box contains dozens of different choices for each facial feature, such as hair, eyebrows, eyes, nose, and mouth. Witnesses who find it difficult to describe a briefly glimpsed face may find it much easier to select from a limited range of visual examples.

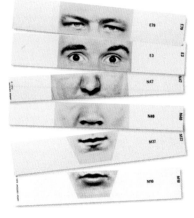

**PHOTO FEATURES**
Commonly called an "identikit," the photo identification system is made up of photos of facial features on strips of card (above). Witnesses trying to recall a face are shown cards for, for instance, the nose. They then pick the one that bears the closest resemblance to the nose they remember. This is assembled with other facial-feature cards to make a composite face (below left).

*Facial jigsaw completed*

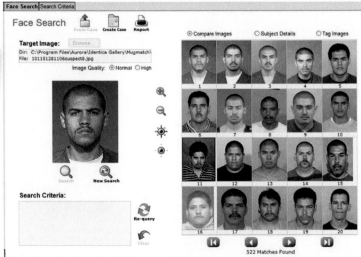

**FINDING POTENTIAL MATCHES**
In those cases where a good image of a suspect has been provided, the computer revolutionizes the task of searching through records to see whether information on the suspect has already been gathered. Here, the image of a suspect appears on the left-hand side of the computer display. On the right side of the screen there are 20 images retrieved by the computer from its database, which it has selected as good matches to the suspect's photograph. The computer can retrieve these matches within a few seconds from a database that may contain millions of faces. It is now up to a human expert to compare the selected images and decide if any of them really do depict the suspect.

44

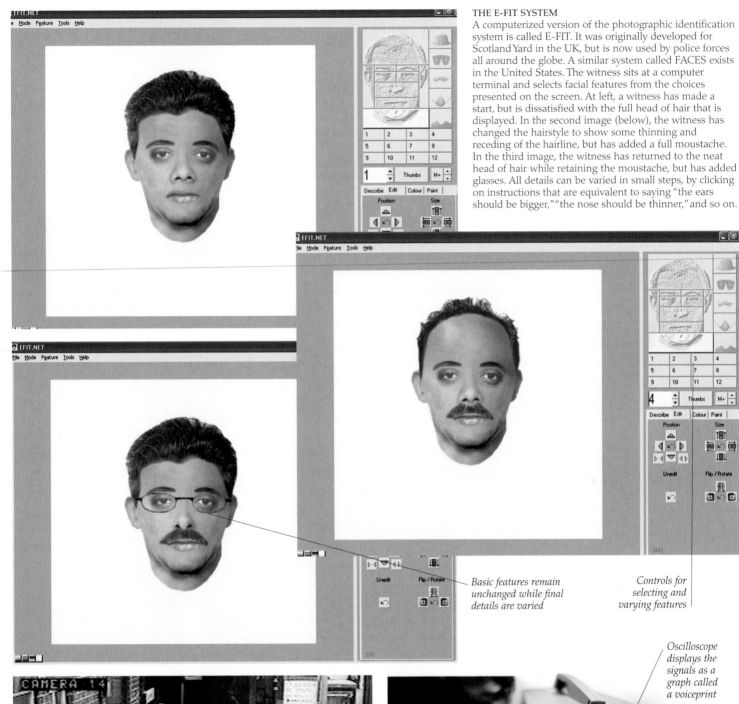

## THE E-FIT SYSTEM

A computerized version of the photographic identification system is called E-FIT. It was originally developed for Scotland Yard in the UK, but is now used by police forces all around the globe. A similar system called FACES exists in the United States. The witness sits at a computer terminal and selects facial features from the choices presented on the screen. At left, a witness has made a start, but is dissatisfied with the full head of hair that is displayed. In the second image (below), the witness has changed the hairstyle to show some thinning and receding of the hairline, but has added a full moustache. In the third image, the witness has returned to the neat head of hair while retaining the moustache, but has added glasses. All details can be varied in small steps, by clicking on instructions that are equivalent to saying "the ears should be bigger," "the nose should be thinner," and so on.

*Basic features remain unchanged while final details are varied*

*Controls for selecting and varying features*

*Oscilloscope displays the signals as a graph called a voiceprint*

*Microphone changes voice sounds into electrical signals*

## CCTV CATCHES TERRORISTS

This CCTV picture shows four inconspicuous-looking men entering a railroad station to travel 30 miles (50 km) to London, England. It could not show the bombs they were carrying in their backpacks, which would soon kill them and 52 others in central London. But this and other pictures afterward provided vital clues to their movements and the terrorist network they belonged to.

## SOUND EVIDENCE

Every person has a unique voice. Forensic phoneticians are speech experts who can deduce a person's age, sex, and race by listening to voice recordings. They may also use voice spectrography. This measures variations in the sound as a person speaks, and produces a graphic representation called a "voiceprint." Like fingerprints, voiceprints can be compared to identify individuals.

# Behavior of the offender

PROFILERS STUDY CRIMES to get a picture of the criminal's personality or way of life. Geographical profiling studies the locations and timings of a series of crimes. Burglars, for example, rarely commit robberies close to their own homes, and travel connections influence the pattern of their robberies. If a burglar lives close to a highway intersection, the most convenient places for him to target are residential districts close to the next intersections along the highway. If he has a legitimate daytime job, he has to commit his burglaries in the evenings and on weekends. Psychological profiling works back from the way the crime is carried out to deduce the criminal's personality and history. Someone who commits violent repeated assaults is more than likely to have displayed a violent personality in the past and to have a police record. Investigators also try to "get inside the mind" of a suspect during interrogation. The "lie detector," or polygraph, is based on the idea that someone who is lying will give themselves away by, for example, increased sweating and raised heart rate. However, in reality, few courts accept polygraph results.

*Scenes of crime*

*Hand-marked map of crimes*

*Highly probable base area of robber*

*Blue band is least likely area for base*

Computer-generated maps of probabilities

## GETTING WARMER
Red dots mark a series of bank robberies in central England (top). A profiler with expertise at geographical profiling was brought in. He came up with a computer map (center) that showed the probable location of the offender's base—his home or where he stored loot. Red areas are the most likely, blue the least. A 3-D version (bottom) shows the red areas as "peaks." The profiler reduced the search area to a tenth of the area covered by the crimes, and the criminal was soon caught.

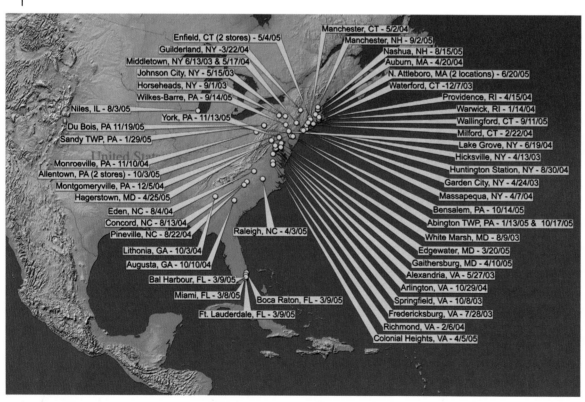

Manchester, CT - 5/2/04
Enfield, CT (2 stores) - 5/4/05
Guilderland, NY -3/22/04
Middletown, NY 6/13/03 & 5/17/04
Johnson City, NY - 5/15/03
Horseheads, NY - 9/1/03
Wilkes-Barre, PA - 9/14/05
Niles, IL - 8/3/05
York, PA - 11/13/05
Du Bois, PA 11/19/05
Sandy TWP, PA - 1/29/05
Monroeville, PA - 11/10/04
Allentown, PA (2 stores) - 10/3/05
Montgomeryville, PA - 12/5/04
Hagerstown, MD - 4/25/05
Eden, NC - 8/4/04
Concord, NC - 8/13/04
Pineville, NC - 8/22/04
Raleigh, NC - 4/3/05
Lithonia, GA - 10/3/04
Augusta, GA - 10/10/04
Bal Harbour, FL - 3/9/05
Miami, FL - 3/8/05
Boca Raton, FL - 3/9/05
Ft. Lauderdale, FL - 3/9/05

Manchester, NH - 9/2/05
Nashua, NH - 8/15/05
Auburn, MA - 4/20/04
N. Attleboro, MA (2 locations) - 6/20/05
Waterford, CT -12/7/03
Providence, RI - 4/15/04
Warwick, RI - 1/14/04
Wallingford, CT - 9/11/05
Milford, CT - 2/22/04
Lake Grove, NY - 6/19/04
Hicksville, NY - 4/13/03
Huntington Station, NY - 8/30/04
Garden City, NY - 4/24/03
Massapequa, NY - 4/7/04
Bensalem, PA - 10/14/05
Abington TWP, PA - 1/13/05 & 10/17/05
White Marsh, MD - 8/9/03
Edgewater, MD - 3/20/05
Gaithersburg, MD - 4/10/05
Alexandria, VA - 5/27/03
Arlington, VA - 10/29/04
Springfield, VA - 10/8/03
Fredericksburg, VA - 7/28/03
Richmond, VA - 2/6/04
Colonial Heights, VA - 4/5/05

## JEWELRY ROBERIES
An FBI map shows the locations and dates of a string of related jewel robberies along the East Coast of the United States that began in April 2003 and continued for some years. In total, over 50 thefts occurred, amounting to over $5 million-worth of stolen jewelry. Creating a map like this is the first step in searching for behavior patterns that might reveal the perpetrators' base, their means of transportation, and perhaps where they will strike next. Even with a smaller number of incidents, this type of map can be helpful.

## CRACKER
A psychological profiler featured in the hit TV series *Cracker* (a slang name for a profiler). The central character, "Fitz" Fitzgerald, was played in the British series by Robbie Coltrane (above), and by Robert Pastorelli in the US remake. Fitz has brilliant insight into the minds of criminals, but also severe personal problems of his own. In reality, the use of profilers is limited: police may listen to a profiler's views, but they keep an open mind. Police rarely work on "hunches," using a trained forensic psychologist to help plan a methodical approach to catching the criminal.

## A PROFILING SUCCESS

In 1956, Dr. James A. Brussel, a psychiatrist, drew up a profile of the "Mad Bomber" who had been terrorizing New York City for years. He said the bomber was a neat and tidy, heavily built male, 40–50 years old, with a serious illness. He perhaps lived with an older female relative. And he might be wearing a double-breasted suit. The police eventually arrested George Metesky (above) at the house where he lived with his two older sisters. He fit the profile—even wearing a double-breasted suit to go to the police station.

Police mugshots of Lee Boyd Malvo

John Allen Muhammad

## A PROFILING FAILURE

On the evening of October 2, 2002, James Martin was shot dead in a grocery store parking lot in Washington, D. C. The following morning, James Buchanan was killed by the same gun. Four more people were killed that day. Over the next three weeks, another four were killed by the "Washington Sniper." The city lived in fear: people avoided shopping or going to garages, and schools kept children inside during breaks. Police profilers tried to figure out the killer's characteristics. They decided that the sniper was most likely a white male in his thirties. On October 24, a suspect car was seen at a highway rest stop. Inside were the killers—two black men, neither in his thirties. The instigator was John Allen Muhammad, aged 41. The younger man was Lee Boyd Malvo.

## DETECTING LIES?

A man is interviewed as he sits hooked up to a polygraph, or "lie-detector," in a police station. Sensors record his pulse rate, blood pressure, breathing rate, and amount of sweating. Measurements are made when he answers "neutral" questions—about, for example, what he had for lunch. These are compared with measurements made when he is asked about the offense. High pulse rate, sweating, or raised blood pressure are taken to indicate nervousness and perhaps guilt.

*Tubes record breathing*

*Fingertip sensor measures sweating*

*Cuff on arm measures blood pressure and pulse*

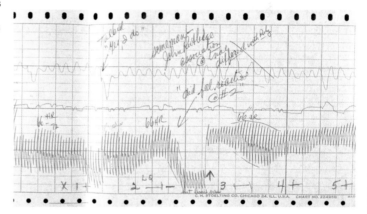

## PORTRAIT OF A KILLER

Jack Ruby was a nightclub owner in Dallas, Texas, in the 1960s. He was also the man who killed President Kennedy's assassin, Lee Harvey Oswald. There was no doubt that Ruby fired the gun, but investigators wanted to know his motive and whether he was part of a gang. His polygraph test (above) was examined for signs of untruthfulness in his story. He died before conviction.

*Readings from "loaded" questions are compared with output from neutral questions to detect contrast*

# Fire starters

WHEN A FIRE HAS THREATENED LIFE or actually killed, forensic investigators move in to answer two main questions: how did it start, and how did it develop to become so damaging? Deliberately starting a fire is called arson. Some people do it for malicious pleasure, others because they have a grudge against the victims, and others to claim insurance on the property. But the great majority of fires start accidentally. The forensic investigators try to find out how the fire progressed once it started, because this can tell them whether dangerous materials played a part. A material that easily catches fire is said to be flammable, and materials sold for construction and furnishings must be nonflammable or have very low flammability. A fire might spread rapidly if a building has been badly designed, so forensic scientists have to keep up to date with the latest developments in architecture and building design, since sometimes these can create new fire hazards.

**AFTERMATH OF FIRE**
This room has been devastated by fire. Heat and smoke have destroyed the windows and all the furniture. The interior will need complete rebuilding if the house is to be used again. If anyone has died, forensic scientists will investigate to decide how the fire started, whether anyone did it deliberately, or whether someone was reckless or negligent. The electric heater in the center of the room will interest investigators.

**SNIFFING FOR CLUES**
After a fire, a forensic investigator uses "sniffing" equipment to search for traces of accelerant—a fluid used to make a fire burn more fiercely. If he finds it, it will suggest that the fire was deliberately started. The most commonly used accelerants are gas, paraffin, and turpentine. The apparatus seen here draws in air close to the area being examined, through the long tube. A miniature automatic chemical lab in the device analyzes the gases in the sample. If the device finds traces of an accelerant, detailed examination of that area begins, and samples are taken away to a forensic laboratory for thorough analysis.

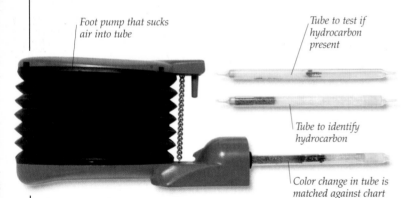

_Foot pump that sucks air into tube_

_Tube to test if hydrocarbon present_

_Tube to identify hydrocarbon_

_Color change in tube is matched against chart_

**GAS ANALYSIS**
This is one type of device used for analyzing gas samples at the scene of a fire. Called a Dräger tube after the German company that first started making instruments of this type, it consists of a foot-operated bellows that sucks air through a transparent tube containing chemicals. Different accelerants cause different color changes at various points along the tube.

**THE THREAT OF FLASHOVER**
Firefighters are trained to recognize signs that warn of imminent trouble. This fire, started artificially in a training area, has reached a dangerous point, called "rollover," in which snakes of flame begin to separate from the main fire. At any moment there is likely to be a "flashover," in which everything flammable in the surrounding area, having become intensely hot, bursts into flame, even without being in contact with the main fire. Forensic fire investigators must do part of their training in simulators like this in order to understand how fires work.

**SPONTANEOUS COMBUSTION**
Stories are often told of "spontaneous human combustion"—people bursting into flame with no apparent cause, as shown in this print from Charles Dickens' novel _Bleak House_. The real explanation, experts believe, is that an unconscious person gets caught in a fire that starts in a normal way.

## EUROPE'S BIGGEST PEACETIME FIRE

A vast column of smoke is seen here rising from a burning oil depot at Buncefield, in southeast England. Described as the biggest fire in Europe since the World War II (1939–1945), it began when automatic equipment overfilled an oil tank with gasoline. The excess flowed into an open reservoir, and a large cloud of gas fumes built up over the unmanned site early on December 11, 2005. The inevitable explosion engulfed more than 20 large storage tanks. No one was killed, but nearby housing was severely damaged, 2,000 people were evacuated, and the oil depot was devastated. Soon, forensic scientists established the sequence of events and ruled out terrorism.

## A BURNED-OUT BUILDING

Many buildings near the Buncefield oil depot were destroyed in the blaze (right), including this house. The total destruction of its interior shows how ferocious, all-consuming, and fast-spreading a fire can be. Although the forensic investigators know the cause of this fire, it is still their responsibility to look for signs that might indicate how and why it spread so far from the main site and why the consequences were so disastrous.

*Smoke plume rose nearly 2 miles (3 km) high*

*Some fires were extinguished, but others were allowed to burn themselves out*

# Fire testing

DISCOVERING THE CAUSE OF A FIRE, why it spread, and why there were casualties can be difficult—which is not surprising, since burning itself is a complex chemical reaction. When a material burns, it combines with oxygen from the air. Heat is released and new substances are formed. These substances include smoke and ash. Invisible gases are also produced, such as potentially lethal carbon monoxide, hydrogen cyanide, and sulfur dioxide. Fires are often fatal. People are killed by the heat, by poisonous gases, and by choking smoke. Dense smoke is also dangerous because it reduces visibility, so that people cannot find their way to escape from the fire. Forensic experts do a huge amount of laboratory work to investigate how materials burn, which materials are dangerous because they combust readily or give off toxic gases, and how buildings can be improved to lessen the risk of fire. Armed with this knowledge, the scientists can advise companies that build and furnish hotels, offices, factories, and shopping centers. Such research also means that forensic scientists are better equipped to understand what actually happened when they investigate in the aftermath of a fire.

**HOW DID IT START?**
Samples of charred debris collected from a fire scene may yield valuable evidence. They are usually examined for traces of accelerant, which would suggest that the fire was a criminal act of arson. The collecting jars are always glass and the lids are made of a specially chosen plastic, neither of which contain chemicals that might contaminate the sample.

*Piece of charred carpet from fire scene*

## HOW MUCH HEAT?
The cone calorimeter is a machine that tests the amount of heat energy materials give out when they burn, and the rate at which it is produced. (The word calorimeter means "heat measurer," and the cone referred to is a cone-shaped heater.) This is important, because the more heat the material gives out, and the quicker it does so, the more intense the fire is and the faster it spreads. The calorimeter subjects a sample to extreme heat until it ignites. A computer then calculates how much energy is released by combustion, and how rapidly.

**1 PREPARING THE SAMPLE**
Here, the material being tested in the cone calorimeter is a type of plastic. A square sample of the plastic is placed on aluminum foil to be mounted in the machine. The foil will reflect heat from the cone onto the sample.

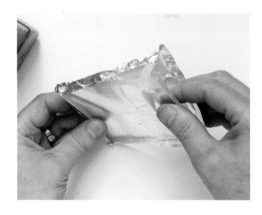

## HOW MUCH SMOKE?
Smoke is a killer, so it is vital to know the smoke-producing properties of materials used in furnishings and construction. This is what the smoke density chamber tests. A sample, such as a piece of carpet, is mounted on a stand (inset). Then a strong electric current is passed through the heating unit, which glows intensely hot. The machine records the time it takes for smoke to be given off by the heated sample and to build up to a maximum. It also measures the amount of smoke produced by detecting how strongly it absorbs light.

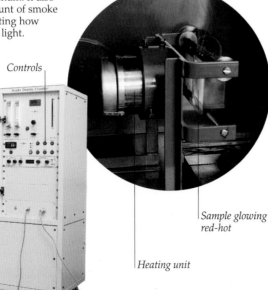

*Sample mount*  *Controls*

*Sample glowing red-hot*

*Heating unit*

*Test chamber*

**2 POSITIONING THE SAMPLE**
The operator mounts the sample in the machine, on the platform near his left hand. Above the sample is the electrically heated cone. A shutter then opens to expose the sample to the cone's intense heat.

**3 IGNITING THE SAMPLE**
As the plastic's temperature rises, it starts to give off hot gases. When the gases are concentrated enough, they are ignited by sparks made by the thin white probe on the left. Sensors detect the energy released.

## HOW EASILY DOES IT BURN?

The oxygen index apparatus measures the flammability of a material (how readily it burns) in terms of the amount of oxygen it needs to ignite. As a fire burns, it uses up the oxygen in a closed space, such as a room or a hallway. At the same time the temperature rises. Most materials will eventually catch fire, despite the falling oxygen level, if the temperature rises high enough. Scientists use a number scale called the oxygen index to describe flammability. The lower the index number, the less oxygen the material needs to ignite, and the more dangerous it is to use in buildings, furnishings, clothing, and other products.

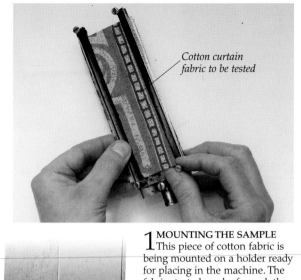

*Cotton curtain fabric to be tested*

### 1 MOUNTING THE SAMPLE

This piece of cotton fabric is being mounted on a holder ready for placing in the machine. The fabrics tested can be from clothes, curtains, or furniture coverings. Other types of material can also be tested—the plastic coating of electrical wires, for example.

### 2 IGNITING THE SAMPLE

The sample is placed inside a strengthened glass tube. Hot air containing a controlled amount of oxygen is piped through the tube. The technician lights the sample with a curved gas lighter. Above the sample is the extractor hood—a chimney that sucks waste gases out of the tube.

*Hood extractor draws off waste gases*

### 3 BURNING THE SAMPLE

At a sufficiently high temperature the sample will burn, even in oxygen-poor air. The machine records the minimum oxygen content needed for combustion—the material's oxygen index number. Cotton, for example, has a relatively high index number of about 18, meaning it can burn in air that contains 18 percent oxygen—normal air is 21 percent oxygen.

*Lighter*

*Control panel*

*Burning sample*

# Crash investigation

A MAJOR INCIDENT IS ALMOST ALWAYS followed by a thorough investigation. A train, plane, ship, or several cars may be involved, and a large number of people hurt or killed. Such disasters are usually the result of many rare events coming together by chance, or they may be an act of terrorism. Whether the cause is accident, carelessness, or sabotage, it is important to find out if anyone is to blame. Perhaps the correct safety and security procedures weren't followed, or maybe there was a design fault or equipment failure in the vehicle. These questions will be decided in court. The job of the forensic experts is to piece together the whole chain of events leading up to the disaster. They're helped by event recorders—"black boxes"—which are installed in airliners, trains, and ships. These hold instrument and voice recordings of everything that goes on in the vehicle's control center.

*Radar showed plane broke up in midair*

*Retrieved fuselage confirms bomb damage*

**EMERGENCY STOP**
The lengths of skid marks, together with a knowledge of the vehicle type and how heavily it was loaded, indicate the speed at which the vehicle was traveling. Weather conditions must also be considered. If skid marks start on the wrong side of the road, they may indicate reckless driving. If they start too close to some stationary obstacle, they indicate the driver was sleepy or not alert.

*Early part of skid mark beginning to show swerve*

*Warning to unauthorized personnel*

*Signals in/out*

*Power supply meter*

**CRASH DUMMY**
This "driver" has been saved from serious damage by the car's seat belt and inflated air bag. Car safety features are tested using crash dummies like this. The results are used not only in building safer cars but also in learning what the results of crashes are, so that forensic investigators can work backward from the aftermath of an accident to what actually happened. Such tests show, for example, that doubling the speed of cars in a collision results in a fourfold increase in damage.

FLIGHT RECORDER DO NOT OPEN

FAIRCHILD

COCKPIT VOICE RECORDER

*Reflective stripes to aid recovery*

*Crash-resistant case*

**LAST WORDS**
This is one of the two flight recorders from a crashed plane. Although called "black boxes," they are always bright red, and tough, to make them easily visible in wreckage. The one shown here is a Cockpit Voice Recorder (CVR), which records conversations among the crew. Current CVRs store the last two hours of conversation. The Flight Data Recorder (FDR) stores data from the plane's instruments.

## PAN AM FLIGHT 103

The shattered body of a Boeing 747 airliner, Pan Am Flight 103, was painstakingly reassembled from hundreds of thousands of parts recovered over a vast area in and around the small town of Lockerbie, in Scotland. On December 21, 1988, the plane exploded on its way from London to New York. All 259 passengers and crew were killed, as well as 11 Lockerbie residents. Forensic scientists discovered that a bomb placed in the hold had torn the plane apart.

Air accident investigator

## OFF THE RAILS

On June 3, 1998, a German Intercity Express train was involved in a catastrophic crash near Eschede. There were 101 dead, and 88 seriously injured. Forensics revealed that a wheel rim had broken due to metal fatigue—a problem foreseen by other train operators, who had altered the design. As the train traveled over a set of points, the displaced wheel hit a trackside lever, changing the points and derailing the rear cars. The train cars hit the pillars of a bridge, which fell onto the train. In complex cases like this, blame and responsibility can be difficult to establish. Although two officials and an engineer from the train company were taken to court, the charges were later dropped.

# The big bang

INSIDE A BOMB, a chemical reaction generates very hot, high-pressure gas that suddenly blasts outward, potentially devastating anything nearby. Gunpowder and similar materials need oxygen from the atmosphere to make the reaction work. This limits their power, so they are called low explosives. High explosives, such as dynamite, already contain the oxygen they need, and are used for a stronger, more rapid blast. A typical bomb contains an easily detonated explosive, called the primary explosive. This in turn triggers a more powerful but harder-to-detonate material, called the secondary explosive. A bomb can be made more deadly by putting it in a tough casing, such as an iron pipe, or by packing shrapnel (nails or other pieces of metal) around the explosive.

**BUS BOMBING**
This double-decker London bus was wrecked by a bomb exploding at the rear of the top deck. The picture shows the devastation that can be inflicted by a quantity of explosive small enough to be contained in a backpack. The bombing was the last of four that took place in London on July 7, 2005. Forensics work established that the bus bomber was among the 16 dead, and that the explosive consisted of homemade materials.

*Fragment of suitcase lining*

CMS        10        20

**SNIFFER DOG**
Here, a dog trained to detect explosives alerts its handler to a suspicious garbage can in Jerusalem, Israel. "Sniffer" dogs like this are taught to sit or bark when they encounter something that smells of explosive. Dogs are more efficient than any sniffer machines developed so far. They are used to search for explosives when an attack is feared, and for traces of explosive after an attack.

**SUITCASE BOMB**
These fragments of a suspect suitcase from the wreckage of Pan Am 103—the airliner that exploded over Lockerbie, Scotland, in 1988—were meticulously gathered and numbered along with thousands of pieces from the plane (see p. 53). After extensive study, investigators decided that the bomb was hidden in a cassette recorder inside this suitcase, which was stowed in the plane's hold. They created controlled explosions in replicas of the hold, filled with luggage, to figure out exactly how strong the explosion was. Fragments of the electronics of the recorder and labels on shreds of clothing led to two men who were eventually charged with the crime.

**THWARTED MISSION**
A bomb placed in a vehicle is hard to detect, and the vehicle can park in a town center without attracting undue attention. These large canisters of gas were removed from a truck that was intended to cause death and destruction in a city in Colombia, South America. The gas is normally used in industry or homes to provide heat and light. The canisters are very strong, to keep the liquefied gas under high pressure. So the bomb included an extra explosive that was capable of cracking the canisters.

*Back of bus
peeled apart*

## BOMB BELT
Although a dummy, this bomb is like a device worn around a suicide bomber's waist. This "bomb" is being used in a training exercise for security guards. A real bomb would be triggered by a switch held in the wearer's hand. A guard attempting to make the bomb safe has the problem of immobilizing the bomber instantly, without giving him or her a chance to trigger the device. A suicide bombing is one of the most difficult kinds of attack to deal with, because there may be nothing suspicious about the bomber except perhaps a bulky jacket. Since the bomber is prepared to die carrying out the attack, intercepting him or her with force may have little effect.

## IMPROVISED BOMB
The hastily constructed bomb below was planted in a mosque in Hyderabad, Pakistan, but it was made safe before exploding. A liquid explosive is stored in the two aluminum flasks. The assembly is wrapped in plastic held together with adhesive tape. Wires to detonate the bomb lead into the cylinders from the circuit board, but are here partly disconnected. A radio signal, most likely from a cell phone, would have set off the electronic switch that triggered the bomb. When a sophisticated trigger mechanism like this is recovered, it often gives more information than any other part of the bomb about the makers.

*Flask containing
liquid explosive*

*Part of
detonating
device*

## TRAP FOR THE UNWARY
This metal box houses a lethal homemade bomb. The explosive, called Semtex, is in the plastic bag on the left. Wires lead to a radio receiver on the right, to which a signal is sent to detonate the bomb. If anyone but an expert had tried to open the box, they would have set off the mousetrap in the center—which also would have triggered the bomb.

*Radio receiver*

*Semtex*

*Mousetrap acts
as a booby-trap*

## COUNTDOWN TO DESTRUCTION
A bomb packed in a plastic box has a deadly extra attached to it—a plastic soft-drink bottle containing gasoline. On the side of the box is an ordinary kitchen timer, which controls the time of detonation. The explosive inside the box scatters the gas and ignites it, making this a potentially devastating incendiary (fire-starting) device.

*Deadly
soft-drink
container*

*Circuit board
triggers bomb
when cell
phone signal
is received*

# Computer forensics

TODAY IT IS POSSIBLE to strike up friendships, do business deals, and buy goods around the globe via the online computer and the cell phone. Crime is expanding fast in this digital world. Vast sums are stolen by criminals accessing someone else's bank account. People can be swindled by spam emails offering fake business propositions. Young people in chat rooms can be drawn into danger by older people posing as teenagers. Terrorists can share their knowledge of bomb making. But dealings in cyberspace are often not as anonymous as the criminals think. Police can find the rough location of a computer user who is visiting a suspect internet site. The position of a cell phone can be roughly localized when it makes a call. Everyone leaves information about themselves in many places, whenever they shop or travel, and the forensic investigator can take advantage of this electronic trail when trying to track down criminals.

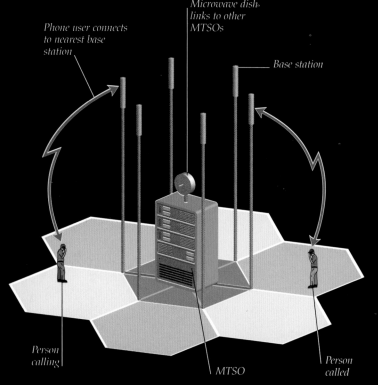

*Phone user connects to nearest base station*

*Microwave dish links to other MTSOs*

*Base station*

*Person calling*

*MTSO*

*Person called*

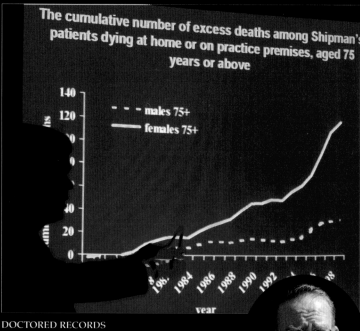

The cumulative number of excess deaths among Shipman's patients dying at home or on practice premises, aged 75 years or above

- - - males 75+
— females 75+

CELL PHONE NETWORK
Cell phones (cell phones) are so called because the phone company divides the area served into a grid of "cells"—areas roughly hexagonal in shape. Each base station (relay mast) is located at the point where three cells meet. Two people holding a phone conversation are each connected to their nearest base station. Base stations communicate through an MTSO (Mobile Telephone Switching Office) to other base stations. The phone company's log shows which base stations were involved in the call, and therefore which cells the callers were in, but not their precise locations.

DOCTORED RECORDS
Tampering with his own computer helped to give away one of the most prolific serial killers, Dr. Harold Shipman (right). The English doctor is believed to have killed about 250 of his elderly patients over at least 30 years. He gave them drug overdoses and had their bodies cremated to hide the evidence. Forensic investigation later showed an unnaturally large number of deaths among his patients—as shown in a graph displayed at an inquiry (above). He also altered the records on his computer to make it seem that he had been giving them proper treatment—not realizing that a copy of the original records remained concealed on the computer's hard drive. Forensic experts discovered these when they examined his computer. Shipman seems to have killed his victims from a desire for power over life and death, but he altered one victim's will to inherit her money, exposing his part in her death.

### COMPUTER DETECTIVE
A police expert is seen here removing the hard drive from a suspect's computer. Investigators have to follow a standard procedure when raiding computers to ensure they do not inadvertently destroy evidence. Any printing must be completed because the criminals might be printing incriminating files before deleting them on the computer. A computer should not be switched on because then it might be accessed remotely and tampered with. The police will sketch or photograph the computers' positions and connections before removing them, and look for written notes containing passwords.

### A VIRUS STRIKES
An unexpected picture on a screen—such as this skull and crossbones—tells the shocked user that a virus has infected the computer. A virus is a malicious program that is spread from computer to computer. At best it causes inconvenience—the skull and message may be all this virus inflicts on the computer. At worst the virus can destroy information or make the computer unusable until major work has been done on it. Thousands of viruses are in circulation via the Internet or shared computer disks, and others are spreading through cell phones. Vast sums are spent on preventing viruses and "curing" infected computers.

*Printed circuit connects with outside world*

### SMART CARD
A smart card, such as the one exploded here, is a credit or debit card that can "remember" information about its user. The "brain" of the card is the microprocessor, or microchip—a tiny complex computer circuit. This "memory chip" encrypts data (translates into a secret code) for utmost securiy. The microchip is glued into a recess in the card. On top of the microchip is the larger printed circuit, which links the microchip to the outside world by connecting to terminals in a cash machine or a card reader in a shop. The microchip can carry information about the cardholder's identity, amount of money in the account, amount he or she is allowed to borrow, and so on. If the card falls into the hands of criminals, they will not be able to access the information unless they also get the user's PIN (personal identification number).

*Front of plastic card*

*Microprocessor or "brain" of card*

*Glue*

*Plastic support*

*Recess*

*Card holder's account number*

# Paper trail

FORENSIC SCIENTISTS OFTEN NEED to make a close examination of a paper document. It might be a blackmail letter or a threatening message, or a forged document such as a faked check. Sometimes a forensics expert compares samples of handwriting to see if the same person wrote them. In the past, when typewriters were widely used, it was possible to identify the machine used by imperfections in the letters typed. Today photocopiers and printers can often be identified by tiny imperfections in the copies. Many now print almost invisible information on their printouts that police can detect. Another kind of document that police often have to examine is paper currency. These days currency designs incorporate many safety features that are hard to fake—but sometimes a forgery is so good that it takes an expert forensic analyst to recognize it.

## PRINTING AND PRIVACY
Many computer printers now print a microscopic code on the pages they output. Governments have requested this information to help the police identify when and where a document was printed. It is especially useful for tracking documents that criminals might create when planning business fraud or terrorism. Office printers can inform managers over the internet whether the printer needs to be repaired or is out of ink or paper. By the same means, it might be possible to say who was using a particular printer.

### MICRO DOTS
The printer "secret code" is in the form of patterns of tiny yellow dots printed all over the page. They show up best through a magnifying glass and under a blue light.

### CODED MESSAGE
This example—enlarged from the sheet of paper above—shows 15 columns by eight rows of dots or gaps. When decoded, it shows the date, time, and printer ID number.

## BANKNOTE ANTIFORGERY FEATURES
Some criminals use high-quality color photocopiers to turn out fake currency. The copies can fool people who are too busy or careless to check that the money is real. But many features of genuine banknotes cannot be reproduced. They are printed on strong, high-quality paper, with their own characteristic "feel." If a cashier draws on the money with a counterfeit-detecting pen, the ink will turn gold if the paper is the right kind, but black if it is not. The designs on a genuine banknote are extremely intricate—a photocopier may blur them. The designs on the front and back are precisely aligned—hard to do on a photocopier.

### SEE-THROUGH REGISTER
When this note is held up to the light, the incomplete "£" symbols on the front and back combine, showing the printing coincides accurately on both sides.

### ULTRAVIOLET FEATURE
A UV banknote-testing lamp shone onto the British 20-pound note makes a large "20" appear in a red and green pattern. Similar patterns appear elsewhere on the note.

### WATERMARK
In this banknote, a "ghostly" watermark—featuring Queen Elizabeth II and the number £20—becomes visible when held up against the light.

### HOLOGRAPHIC STRIP
A series of foil patches forms a line. When you turn the note to catch the light at different angles, a face or the symbols "£" and "20" appears.

### QUALITY
Banknotes have a special "feel," because of the heavy, high-quality paper used. Forgers use cheaper papers that are easily detectable.

### MICROLETTERING
A magnifying glass reveals tiny lettering beneath the Queen: the value of the note in letters ("TWENTY") and numerals ("20").

### RAISED PRINT
A finger run across the note can feel raised print in some areas, such as in the words "Bank of England" and on the figure "20" bottom right.

## ELECTROSTATIC DETECTIVE

Forensic investigators can sometimes find traces of writing on a sheet of paper—even though they are invisible to the naked eye. When someone writes on the top sheet of a pad, a copy of the writing is left in the form of very slight impressions (dents) in the sheets beneath. The impression is greatest on the next sheet down, but if the writer presses hard, marks may be left on several sheets. The ESDA (Electrostatic Detection Apparatus) is a high-tech way of making the impressions on a lower sheet visible.

### 1 APPLYING THE FILM
The investigator lays the sheet of paper being investigated on a porous metal plate forming the top of the ESDA device. There are small holes in the plate. A pump sucks air through the holes, pulling the film and paper hard against the plate, in order to make a good contact between them.

### 2 CHARGING THE FILM
The operator waves a "wand," which is an electrode connected to a power supply at a very high voltage. This produces an electric charge all over the film (like static in hair). The charge is stronger where an impression in the paper creates a slight gap between film and paper.

### 3 SCATTERING THE TONER
The operator scatters powder, like the toner in photocopiers over the charged film, and then blows away the excess. Some powder remains, clinging to the film where the charge is strongest and revealing the writing (see right).

*Fragile scrolls fell to pieces when found*

### THE DEAD SEA SCROLLS
Between 1947 and 1960, a treasure trove of Jewish religious writings was discovered in caves around the Dead Sea in the Middle East. Some were versions of parts of the Bible. But were they genuine, and how could the experts find out their exact age? Carbon dating was the technique used. This measures the radioactive carbon in the scrolls. It showed that the scrolls were written at various dates from the 2nd century BCE to the 1st century CE. Forgery was therefore ruled out.

### THE FÜHRER FORGERIES
In 1981, a German journalist (far left) told his boss about some diaries supposedly written by Hitler. Handwriting experts and a historian declared them authentic. The journalist's magazine and a British newspaper paid millions of dollars to publish extracts. But forensics experts found the paper, inks, and bindings were modern and not available in Hitler's day. The forger and his accomplice, the journalist, were jailed.

*Toner in grooves reveals writing*

# Every picture tells a story

GENUINENESS MAKES ALL THE DIFFERENCE to the value of an artwork. Even an inferior picture by a famous artist will fetch a higher price than an excellent one with an artist's signature that happens to be a fake. Forensic scientists study suspect paintings under light of various wavelengths. A forger might make a picture look convincing to the naked eye but X-rays and infrared light do not deceive. A forger has to be extremely talented and dedicated to produce an "old" picture without resorting to any modern materials.

Among the most notorious forgers of recent years are the Dutchman Han Van Meegeren and Londoner Tom Keating, who both managed to escape detection for a long time. With the development of sophisticated forensic science techniques, it has become easier to spot fakes. Paintings are not the only forms of art that are copied—photographs, ceramics, statues, and other artifacts have hoodwinked the experts.

**MASTER FORGER**
Tom Keating claimed to have painted 2,000 forged paintings during his lifetime. He felt that paintings in his own name did not get the recognition they deserved. He produced paintings in very varied styles, from the 16th century to the 20th. Only bad health saved him from being tried and perhaps jailed. He claimed that he always gave clues that experts should recognize—for example, by using modern paints, or putting historical errors into scenes. Remarkably, his paintings—including the forgeries—have increased in value ever since he was exposed.

**VAN MEEGEREN PAINTING**
Investigators decided that this picture, painted in the style of the 17th-century painter Vermeer, was one of many fakes painted by the forger Han Van Meegeren. Unusually, he was desperate to prove he was guilty of forgery—to prove that he was not guilty of treason. After World War II (1939–1945) he was accused of selling masterpieces to the Nazi invaders of his country. He had to paint a fake picture for the court to prove he had the skill to forge the old pictures. Although found innocent of treason, he was convicted of forgery but died before starting his sentence.

**LOOKING FOR THE INVISIBLE**
A technician aims a powerful spotlight (with a tungsten element) at an oil painting. The lamp illuminates the picture with both visible light (forming the bright patch on the painting) and infrared light, which is invisible radiation with wavelengths longer than those of visible light. The camera is loaded with special thermal imaging film that is sensitive to the infrared light reflected from the picture. In the photograph, details not visible in ordinary light, such as corrections and alterations, will show up. Infrared can also help determine whether the paint used is characteristic of a particular artist, and the picture is therefore genuine. X-rays, which penetrate beneath the surface of the painting, can see whether cracking occurs through all the layers—if it doesn't, the painting is probably a fake.

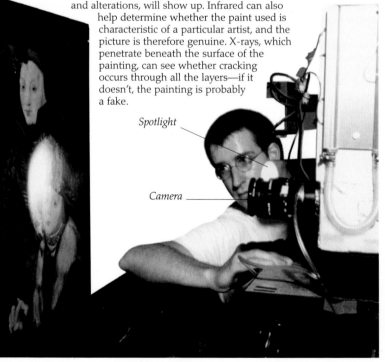

*Spotlight*

*Camera*

## COTTINGLEY FAIRIES

Ten-year-old Frances Griffiths gazes dreamily at a troupe of fairies dancing in the garden. This photograph, taken by her 16-year-old cousin Elsie Wright in 1917, became world famous when published three years later. Many longed to believe these were real fairies—including Sir Arthur Conan Doyle, creator of the great detective Sherlock Holmes (see p. 9). Journalists questioned the girls to find out if the pictures were faked. Using a camera lent by an expert on the paranormal, the girls produced three more pictures of fairies. The images were said to have been retouched (altered) to make them clearer when printed in newspapers and magazines. This accounted for the flat, unconvincing look of the fairies. Many years later, Elsie and Frances admitted that the "fairies" were paper cutouts of pictures copied from a book.

## STORED ENERGY

This African figurine is made of terra-cotta (baked clay). It could be several hundred years old, and may be very valuable. Measuring thermoluminescence (TL) can determine its age, and confirm its value. Clay continually stores energy from natural radioactivity—radiation from substances such as uranium that occur naturally in the ground. When a potter bakes the clay, this energy is released and the buildup of energy starts again. If a forensic scientist later heats a sample of the figure's clay, the stored energy is given out as light. The amount of TL shows how many years have passed since the potter made the figure.

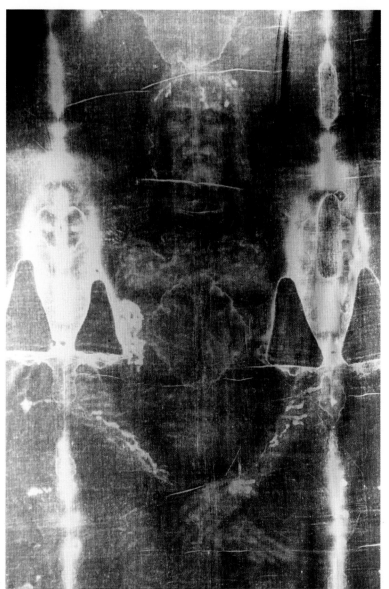

*Shroud sample wrapped in foil*

*Sealed container in which sample was sent for testing*

*Wax seal of the Archbishop of Turin*

## THE TURIN SHROUD

For centuries, this linen cloth (left) was venerated as the shroud in which Jesus was wrapped when taken down from the Cross. The cloth's image of a man's body was said to have been made either miraculously or by some natural process. Fragments from the edge of the cloth have been sent to independent laboratories for analysis. Three radiocarbon dating tests place the cloth somewhere between 1260 and 1390 CE. However, the uncertainties in precisely dating a tiny piece of cloth taken from such a much-handled object are enormous.

# Future forensics

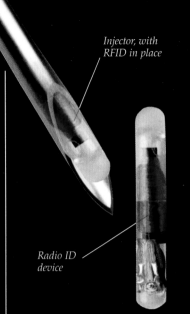

*Injector, with RFID in place*

*Radio ID device*

**S**CIENCE WILL OFFER AN IMPRESSIVE ARRAY of new techniques to police and forensic investigators in the near future. These can increase surveillance over our daily lives, helping the police to detect and solve crime. It will be possible to follow suspects by tracking their travel, their shopping, and their phone calls. From information hidden in digital photos, computer printouts, and computer drives police will be able to figure out a person's movements. Suspects will carry ID that can't be forged—in "biometric" details, such as facial features and eye patterns. Today, in most countries, such information is held only for those who have had a brush with the law. In the future, it may be gathered for everyone from birth. But is this desirable? There is a delicate balance between keeping tabs on criminals to combat crime and the state controlling the freedom of the individual.

*Computer converts iris details into a code*

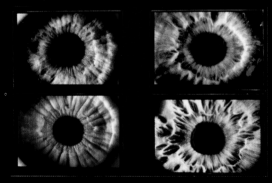

## UNDER THE SKIN

A radio frequency identification device (RFID) is a tiny implant that is inserted under a person's skin using the injector in order to keep track of his or her movements. Some criminals who are on probation and restricted to their homes at certain times already wear bulky radio-tagging devices. One day perhaps they will have these tiny implants, instead, so that the authorities can monitor where they are at all times.

## IRIS SCANNING

This computer screen image is of the iris of an eye being scanned for personal identification. The iris is the colored area around the black central pupil and is unique in each person. A low-power laser beam is shone into the eye. The scanner analyzes the iris into eight circular areas to pick out details. The information about markings in each circle is broken down into a sequence of light and dark patches (inset) and then stored as numbers in a database. It is possible to fake the iris pattern—for example, by wearing special contact lenses with an image of iris patterns printed on them. However, there are ways of detecting this kind of fraud. (In the imaginary future of the science-fiction film, *Minority Report,* eye-scanners are everywhere. To change identity, a character has to have new eyes implanted. Few criminals today would go that far!) Iris scanning will identify someone correctly, but this is useful only when this identity links to a database filled with records showing past or possible criminal activity. Even then, the records' accuracy could be undermined by officials accidentally processing the data incorrectly, or by criminals deliberately altering the data.

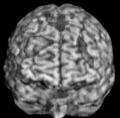

Back view

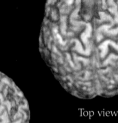

*Most lying activity in frontal area*

Top view

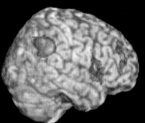

Right side

## THE LYING BRAIN

Functional magnetic resonance imaging (fMRI) is used in medicine to observe how the brain works. The yellow and red areas above show brain cell activity during speech. The person being scanned was asked sometimes to lie and sometimes to tell the truth, while the activity of the brain was observed. Maybe one day police will be able to use a compact brain scanner that can show if a suspect is lying while being interrogated.

## IRIS TYPES

Each iris is full of detail that is particular to each individual and more graphic than a fingerprint. The patterns are consistent throughout life, like fingerprints. A computer can analyze the iris patterns, search on a database, and make a match—or report that there is no match—within 3 seconds.

*Standard set of points measured*

*Face shape scanned into computer*

## MAPPING THE FACE

A face can be scanned and its features summarized in a set of biometric measurements. A mesh of lines is projected in infrared light onto a face and a computer analyzes the way they're curved by underlying facial features. The distance between the centers of the eyes, the ends of the mouth, the length of the nose, and so on are measured rapidly. Facial recognition can be used as security passes as well as for locating criminals. However, as a person ages, facial features change and making a match becomes more difficult.

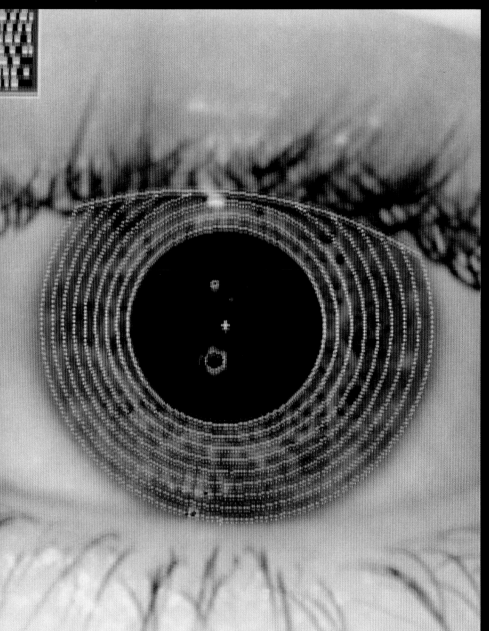

## TRACKING THE TRAFFIC

Clusters of CCTV cameras high above a London street survey and make a record of the vehicles going past. The cameras are linked to computers that can "read" the license numbers. The cameras are at the entrance and exit points of the London congestion-charge zone. Hundreds of thousands of drivers pay a toll to enter the city each day from Monday to Friday. If a car's license goes onto the computer and the owner has not paid the charge, he or she will get a fine in the mail. Such charging may spread to the nation's highways and help to reduce the volume of traffic, while at the same time giving police a way of tracking vehicle movements around the country—modern criminals are highly mobile.

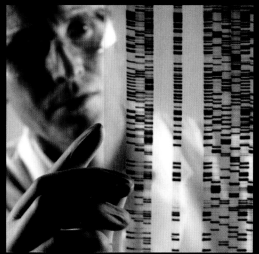

## PERSONAL PROFILE

This scientist is examining DNA profiles. Soon it may be possible to get a DNA profile of a suspect as quickly as a breathalyzer test can detect alcohol in the blood. DNA databases are being built up in many countries, and often there are proposals to extend testing to the whole population. There is a danger that the public will think DNA testing is infallible and that it threatens only the guilty. Criminals know they can confuse DNA evidence by placing other people's DNA at the scene of crime. For example, scattering other people's cigarette butts to point the blame elsewhere. That's why forensic science can never stand still!

# Hall of Fame

**T**HE MAJOR PIONEERS AND CONTRIBUTORS to forensic science have come from many walks of life. Most are scientists, or police officers and detectives. Thanks to their work, there are now crime laboratories and databases all over the world, and forensics plays a key part in the criminal justice system, often providing evidence to convict the guilty and acquit the innocent.

### ABAGNALE , FRANK 1948–
As a teenager, Abagnale taught himself the art of fraud and forgery and started writing checks. He ran away from home at the age of 16, and headed for New York. In a five-year crime spree he conned banks out of more than $2.5 million while posing as an airline pilot, doctor, lawyer, and teacher. By the time of his capture in 1969 Abagnale was wanted in 21 countries. However,

Frank Abagnale's incredible criminal career became the subject of a film in 2002

he served less than five years in prison when the FBI released him on the condition that he help them in their fight against fraud. He later founded his own security consultancy firm and became a legitimate millionaire.

### BALTHAZARD, VICTOR 1872–1950
Balthazard was a professor of forensic medicine at the Sorbonne University in Paris, France. He made a comprehensive forensic study of hair, conducted research into bloodstain patterns, and used photographic enlargements of bullets and cartridge cases to determine weapon type. He was one of the first to attempt to match a bullet to a weapon.

### BELL, JOSEPH 1837–1911
Dr. Bell was a professor at the medical school of the University of Edinburgh, Scotland, where one of his pupils was Arthur Conan Doyle. Bell had a habit of deducing a patient's occupation and history from studying his or her physical details. Conan Doyle used this trait for his fictional detective Sherlock Holmes. Bell's emphasis on close observation also made him a pioneer in his own field, forensic pathology.

### BERTILLON, ALPHONSE 1853–1914
French detective and creator of anthropometry, the science of measuring the body. See pp. 8–9.

### CRICK, FRANCIS 1916–2004
British codiscoverer, with James Watson, of the structure of DNA. See p. 22.

### CRIPPEN, DR. HAWLEY HARVEY 1862–1910
American murderer captured by the use of new wireless communication. See p. 40.

### DNA DATABASE 1995
The world's first DNA database was begun in Britain, and it is still the largest of any country. It holds DNA samples of around 3.5 million convicted criminals and suspects. Continuing technical advances in DNA collection and searching enable police to make new prosecutions for previously unsolved crimes, and to free those wrongly imprisoned.

### FBI, 1908–
The Federal Bureau of Investigation, founded in 1908 as the Bureau of Investigation, under US President Theodore Roosevelt. See Hoover, J. Edgar.

### GALTON, SIR FRANCIS 1822–1911
A cousin of Charles Darwin, Francis Galton was the author of *Fingerprints*. The book showed that fingerprints are individual and permanent, and it established a first classification system, referred to as Galton's Details. This Victorian polymath also worked in statistics, psychology, geography, exploration, and meteorology.

### GLAISTER, SIR JOHN 1856–1932
Scottish professor of forensic medicine and expert witness. See p. 20.

### GODDARD, CALVIN 1891–1955
A pioneer in ballistics, Goddard headed the Bureau of Forensic Ballistics, the US's first independent crime laboratory. The Bureau took on fingerprinting, trace evidence, and blood analysis as well as ballistics. He encouraged the use of the newly invented comparison microscope to identify bullet markings, and was an expert witness at criminal trials.

### GROSS, HANS 1847–1915
Gross was an examining magistrate and professor of criminal law at the University of Graz, Austria. His book *Criminal Investigation* explored the ways that physical evidence can be used to solve crimes He established the Institute of Criminology in Graz .

### HAUPTMANN, BRUNO 1889–1936
This one-time criminal entered the US illegally from his native Germany in 1923. He lived quietly until 1935, when he was accused of the kidnapping and murder of the baby son of famous aviator Charles Lindbergh. "The trial of the century" convicted Hauptmann, partly because of similarities between his signature and a ransom note. But doubts about Hauptmann's guilt remained and, in 2005, three forensic document experts reexamined the handwriting evidence. All independently concluded that Hauptmann was indeed the author of the ransom note.

### HERSCHEL, WILLIAM 1833–1918
British colonial magistrate and the first to use fingerprints for identification. See p. 18.

### HOOVER, J. EDGAR
Founder and controversial director of the FBI in its present form, Hoover held this post for 48 years. The FBI investigates crimes and gathers intelligence about potential criminal activity. Hoover established forensics at the organization by setting up a fingerprint file, a crime laboratory, and the FBI National Academy for training elite officers. The headquarters in Washington, D. C., are named after him.

### IAFIS 1999
The Integrated Automatic Fingerprint Identification System is the US's national fingerprint and criminal history system, and is maintained by the FBI. Submission, storage, and search are integrated in this one electronic

Hauptmann's signature

Composite signature made from ransom note

J. Edgar Hoover, founder of the FBI

system, so that fingerprint checks, which used to take months, can be made in just hours. The IAFIS's database contains the fingerprints and criminal records of more than 47 million people.

**KEATING, TOM 1917–1984**
Successful British art forger. See p. 60.

**KGB 1917–1991**
The KGB was the Soviet Union's secret police. Its goal was to gather foreign intelligence and to pursue the state's enemies, often to the death. The organization used a mix of forensic science, new technology, and old-fashioned coercion to achieve its goals. When the Soviet Union was disbanded, so was the KGB.

**JEFFRIES, SIR ALEC 1950–**
British discoverer of DNA fingerprinting. See p. 22.

**LACASSAGNE, ALEXANDRE 1844–1921**
Sometimes referred to as the founder of forensic science, Lacassagne was a professor of forensic medicine at the University of Lyon, France, where one of his students was the future forensics start Edmond Locard. Lacassagne participated in criminal investigations and was an expert witness at criminal trials. He was the first to study bloodstain pattern analysis and bullet markings.

**LANDSTEINER, KARL 1868–1943**
Austrian discoverer of ABO blood groups and Nobel Prize winner. See p. 20.

**LOCARD, DR. EDMOND 1877–1966**
French forensic scientist most famous for his exchange principle. See p. 27.

**MARKOV, GEORGI 1929–1978**
Bulgarian dissident murdered with a poisoned umbrella. See p. 41.

**MARSH, JAMES 1794–1896**
British chemist who in 1836 devised a test for detecting arsenic, called the "Marsh test." Before the test, colorless, odorless arsenic was untraceable. The poison was used so widely to bump off family members that it became

known as "inheritance powder." Marsh was also a skilled inventor.

**ORFILA, MATHIEU 1787–1853**
Orfila was born in Spain but lived most of his life in Paris, France, where he was a professor of chemistry. He is the author of the influential *Treatise of General Toxicology*, published when he was just 26. The book detailed new techniques for detecting arsenic—a poison frequently used in murder cases—in the body. This, and other works, earned Orfila the title "the father of toxicology."

**OSBORN, ALBERT SHERMAN 1858–1946**
The author of *Questioned Documents* (1910), Osborn devoted his time to analyzing forged documents for more than 50 years. He was an expert witness in many important cases. In 1942 he founded the American Society of Questioned Document Examiners. He also designed a comparison microscope.

**PARKER, ELLIS 1871–1940**
Often described as America's real-life Sherlock

Ellis Parker (right) discusses a case with his son, Ellis Parker Junior

Holmes, Ellis Parker was a Chief of Detectives in New Jersey for 45 years. He helped to solve more than three hundred violent crimes using a forensic mixture of close observation, deduction, and psychology. He became known for spotting details that other missed, and for asking questions that seemed pointless but which often led to an important discovery.

**SCOTLAND YARD, 1829–**
The headquarters for London's Metropolitan Police, founded in 1829 by Sir Robert Peel with the help of Eugène François Vidocq. The Met was an early adopter of forensic science and set up the Fingerprint Branch in 1901, using the Henry System of Classification.

**STARRS, JAMES E.**
American forensic anthropologist James E. Starrs has directed more than 20 exhumations of controversial murderers to try and discover new evidence. The remains of

Wild West gunslinger Jesse James and "Boston strangler" Albert de Salvo have been examined by Starrs. His 2005 book *A Voice for the Dead* detailed his forensic researches. He is a professor of law and forensic science, and writes and edits the journal *Scientific Sleuthing Review*.

**SURETE NATIONALE 1812–**
The French National Police was founded by a former criminal, Eugène François Vidocq, in 1812, under Emperor Napoleon I. The Sûreté Nationale was the criminal investigative bureau of the Paris police, and most of its members—many of them former criminals—worked undercover. The science of secrecy was a huge success and the Paris crime rate was cut by 40 percent in eight years. Today, the Sûreté Nationale is known as the Police Nationale.

**UHLENHUTH, PAUL 1870–1957**
This German bacteriologist devised a test for distinguishing blood from other liquids, and one for distinguishing human blood from other animals' blood. See p. 20.

**VUCETICH, JUAN 1858–1925**
Argentine police officer and anthropologist Juan Vucetich made the first prosecution based on fingerprint evidence, in a murder case. He developed a method of fingerprint classification that would be used by police forces all over the world. In 1904 Vucetich became the director of the Center for Dactyloscopy (fingerprint identification) in Buenos Aires.

**WATSON, JAMES 1928–**
British Nobel Prize winner and codiscoverer, with Francis Crick, of DNA's structure. See p. 22.

Forensic scientist James E. Starrs examines DNA sequences

# Timeline of forensic firsts

Forensic science has long been a weapon in the fight against crime, but today it is used more frequently, and more precisely, than ever before. Early breakthroughs included subjects as diverse as medicine, optics, and handwriting analysis. This timeline tracks the most significant of those advances.

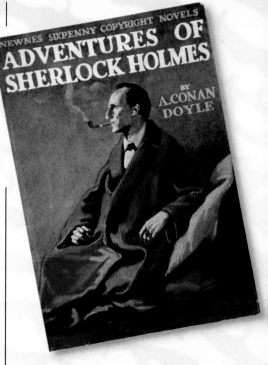

Published in 1892, this collection contained 12 of Holmes's adventures

**1247**
In China the first book on forensic science appears, called *The Washing Away of Wrongs*. Author Sung Tzuh, a lawyer, includes instructions on how to distinguish between suicide, murder, and natural deaths.

**1609**
The first study of handwriting analysis, by François Demelle, is published in France.

**1642**
The University of Leipzig in Germany begins a course on forensic medicine.

**1670**
The first powerful precision microscope is invented by Dutch scientist Anton van Leeuwenhoek. The device will become a vital tool for forensic scientists.

**1776**
During the Revolutionary War, the corpse of General Warren is identified by his false tooth, which was made from a walrus tusk.

**1794**
In Lancashire, Britain, murderer John Toms is convicted on the basis of a torn scrap of paper found on his victim matching a piece in Toms' pocket.

**1804**
German physicist Johann Wilhelm Ritter discovers ultraviolet radiation, which will be used to reveal trace evidence invisible in normal light.

Early precision microscope

**1812**
The world's first detective force, the Sûreté Nationale, is established in Paris, France. It becomes a model for Britain's Scotland Yard and the US's FBI.

**1813**
The influential book *Treatise of Toxicology* by Spanish doctor Mathieu Orfila is published.

**1823**
Czech physiologist Johann Evangelista Purkinje publishes a description of fingerprint types.

**1828**
Scottish physicist William Nicol invents the polarizing light microscope, which will become used for detecting trace evidence.

**1835**
British police officer Henry Goddard studies bullet markings, and demonstrates that a bullet can be matched to the gun that fired it.

**1836**
British chemist James Marsh devises a test for detecting minute quantities of arsenic in the body. The test is soon being used successfully in murder trials.

**1841**
The first detective story, *The Murders in the Rue Morgue* by American author Edgar Allen Poe, is published. From now on, developments in forensic science will be reflected in the adventures of fictional detectives.

**1843**
The first mugshots of suspects are taken by Brussels police in Belgium.

**1850**
In the US, murderer John Webster becomes the first to be convicted by medical evidence when doctors are able to determine the age, sex, and time of death of his victim.

**1856**
In India, administrative officer Sir William Herschel begins to use thumbprints on documents to identify illiterates.

**1859**
The US becomes the first country to allow photographs to be used as evidence in courts of law.

**1861**
In Germany, professor of pathological anatomy Rudolph Virchow makes a study of the value of hair as physical evidence.

**1878**
The Criminal Investigation Department (CID) is Britain's first plain-clothes detective force. The CID is controlled by Scotland Yard.

**1880s**
Italian criminologist Cesare Lombroso measures changes in blood volume to discover if any physiological changes are associated with lying.

**1882**
Anthropometry, a system of bodily measurements, starts to be used as a means of identifying criminals in Paris, France. It will become used by police forces all over the world.

**1883**
American humorist Mark Twain's book *Life on the Mississippi* features the identification of a murderer by fingerprints.

**1887**
Arthur Conan Doyle's *A Study in Scarlet*, the first story featuring Sherlock Holmes, is published in the UK. Holmes goes on to appear in four novels and 56 short stories and become the world's most popular fictional detective.

**1891**
Argentinian police officer Juan Vucetich makes the first criminal identification using fingerprints. As a result, a murderer is convicted. The following year, the Argentinian police force becomes the world's first to use fingerprinting as a means of criminal identification.

**1892**
*Fingerprints*, by British scientist Francis Galton, is first published. The book establishes a classification system, and shows that fingerprints are not inherited, and that even the prints of identical twins are different.

**1893**
The book *System der Kriminalistik* by German forensic scientist Hans Gross covers microscopy, serology, fingerprints, and ballistics. It appears in English in 1907 as *Criminal Investigation*.

**1894**
In France, Captain Alfred Dreyfus is wrongly convicted of treason by an incorrect handwriting identification by expert Alphonse Bertillon. The scandal rocks French politics.

**1895**
German physicist Wilhelm Conrad Röntgen discovers X-rays, which will earn him a Nobel Prize in Physics. X-rays will become a key tool for forensic anthropologists and odontologists.

**1896**
In Britain, Sir Edward Richard Henry publishes *Classification and Uses of Fingerprints*, which establishes a fingerprint classification system that will come to be used across Europe and North America.

**1898**
German chemist Paul Jeserich gets a killer convicted by firing a bullet from a suspect's gun and matching it with one from the crime scene.

**1901**
Austrian pathologist Karl Landsteiner demonstrates three blood types, leading to the ABO system of blood typing.

**1901**
German scientist Paul Uhlenhuth devises the precipitin test, which distinguishes human blood from the blood of other animals.

**1902**
Burglar Harry Jackson is the first person in the UK to be convicted by fingerprint evidence.

**1904**
In Germany, the precipitin test is first used in a criminal court, to convict brutal murderer Ludwig Tessnow.

**1910**
*Questioned Documents* by American document examiner and handwriting expert Albert Osborn is published. The book is still consulted by experts today.

**1910**
The world's first forensic laboratory is opened in France by Edmond Locard.

A record of a suspect's fingerprints

**1911**
Murderer Thomas Jennings is hanged after being convicted by fingerprint evidence in Chicago.

**1913**
Victor Balthazard, professor of forensic medicine at the University of Sorbonne, Paris, publishes an article detailing how bullet markings make every bullet unique.

**1916**
In the US, Albert Schneider uses a vacuum apparatus to collect trace evidence.

**1920**
French forensic expert Edmond Locard formulates his exchange principle, usually summarised as "every contact leaves a trace".

**1920**
An international catalog of firearms is begun by Charles E. Thwaite in the US. Five years later, the collection is complete and any bullet can be matched to the gun that fired it.

**1920**
Physicist John Fisher invents a device called a helixometer, for recording the interiors of gun barrels.

**1920**
American Luke May is the first to study how striation marks on tools can be compared and used as evidence.

**1920**
*The Mysterious Affair at Styles* is published in the US. Agatha Christie's first novel introduces the Belgian detective Hercule Poirot. He will feature in 33 novels and 54 short stories, and in many films.

**1921**
The first lie detector test, or polygraph, is invented by John Larson in the US. The machine measures blood pressure and rate of breathing.

**1923**
A US court rules that polygraph tests are not admissible as evidence.

**1923**
The US's first independent crime laboratory, The Bureau of Forensic Ballistics, opens for business.

**1924**
In the US, two killers are convicted when experts showed that one of them owned the typewriter used to write a ransom note.

**1924**
Los Angeles Chief of Police August Vollmer opens the US's first police crime laboratory.

**1925**
The first comparison microscope, important for matching bullet and other markings, is invented in the US by Philip Gravelle and Calvin Goddard.

**1926**
In the US, Italian-born laborers Nicola Sacco and Bartolomeo Vanzetti are convicted for robbery and murder, largely by ballistics evidence from the new comparison microscope.

**1929**
In Chicago, one of the hitmen responsible for gunning down seven mobsters in the St. Valentine's Day Massacre is identified when guns at his home are matched to cartridge cases from the crime scene.

The presence of maggots can help determine time of death

**1930s**
Mexico introduces the first test to identify gunshot residue on skin, the dermal nitrate test.

**1930**
In the US, the National Fingerprint File is started by the FBI.

**1930**
The *American Journal of Police Science* is founded and published by staff of the Bureau of Forensic Ballistics.

**1932**
The FBI opens its own crime lab, the Technical Crime Laboratory.

**1936**
In a murder trial, Scottish doctor Alexander Mearns uses the life cycle of maggots to estimate the time of the victim's death.

**1936**
Handwriting evidence helps convict German-born murderer Bruno Hauptmann in the US.

**1941**
The voice spectrograph is invented by researchers at Bell Laboratories in the US. The device is intended to identify suspects from speech characteristics.

**1945**
The "Drunkometer," forerunner of the modern Breathalyzer, is developed by Dr. R.N. Harger of Indiana University.

**1948**
The American Academy of Forensic Sciences (AAFS) is founded, to bring together forensic scientists working in different disciplines.

**1950**
Tape lift method of collecting trace evidence is developed by Swiss criminalist Max Frei-Sulzer.

**1953**
Cambridge scientists James Crick and Francis Watson announce that they have discovered the double-helix structure of DNA.

**1954**
The breathalyzer, which estimates alcohol content in the blood from a sample of breath, is invented by Robert Borkenstein in the US. The device will be adopted by police departments around the world.

**1959**
A color test for gunshot residue is developed. Named the Harrison and Gilroy test after its inventors, the test is simpler and clearer than previous ones.

**1965**
In Britain, a team at Cambridge University develops the first scanning electron microscope (SEM). SEMs produce high-resolution 3-D images for analyzing samples in incredible detail.

**1967**
In the US, the FBI opens the National Crime Information Center to coordinate information about criminals and stolen goods.

Fibers in a needle's eye, as seen by a scanning electron microscope

**1971**
French photographer Jacques Penry creates the Photo-FIT ID System, capable of creating 15 billion different faces.

**1975**
The FBI introduces the Automated Fingerprint Identification System (AFIS).

**1977**
In Japan, trace evidence examiner Masato Soba discovers super-glue fuming—a method of revealing latent (hidden) fingerprints.

**1978**
The electrostatic detection apparatus (ESDA) is invented by British scientists Bob Freeman and Doug Foster. The device reveals impressions of handwriting in paper.

**1983**
The so-called Hitler Diaries, bought by the German news magazine *Stern*, are shown to be a fake by forensic document examiners.

**1984**
British geneticist Sir Alec Jefffreys discovers DNA fingerprinting, which uses variations in the genetic code to identify an individual.

**1986**
Polymerase Chain Reaction (PCR), a method of duplicating parts of the DNA molecule, is developed by American chemist Kary Mullis. PCR enables identifications to be made from a minute sample of DNA.

**1988**
In Britain, DNA fingerprinting is used to solve a crime for the first time. It exonerates a murder suspect, and then it nails the real culprit, Colin Pitchfork.

**1989**
In the US, Gary Dotson becomes the first person to have a conviction overturned by DNA evidence. He had served eight years in prison.

**1991**
University College Hospital, London, develops a laser scanning technique that enables a computer simulation of a human face based on the skull's shape.

**1992**
The FBI launches Drugfire, a firearms identification database that stores details of markings for search and comparison to find out if crimes were committed using the same weapons.

**1993**
75 years after their assassination, the remains of the last Russian czar, Nicholas II, and his family are positively identified by comparing samples of DNA from bone tissue with close relatives.

**1994**
The UK Home Office publishes a report called *CCTV: Looking Out For You*, which paves the way for a huge increase in the use of Closed Circuit Television cameras in

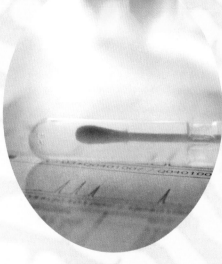

DNA sample on a swab

public places. The UK now has one CCTV camera for every 14 people.

**1995**
The world's first DNA database, containing the DNA records of convicted criminals, is set up in Britain. Other countries will soon follow suit.

**1998**
In the US, professor Don Foster helps police find serial bomber Ted Kaczynski through the new forensic science of literary analysis—studying documents the killer had written to discover who and where he was.

**1999**
The National Integrated Ballistics Network replaces the FBI's Drugfire database. It is a computer network containing digital images of ballistics evidence.

**1999**
The AFIS is integrated to create the Integrated Automated Fingerprint Identification System, making searching for matches much faster.

**2000**
The first episode of *CSI: Crime Scene Investigation* is broadcast on TV in the US. The program shows crimes being solved entirely by a team of forensic investigators. *CSI* will be a huge hit worldwide, and many other dramas about forensic science will follow. Experts complain that the "CSI Effect" gives the public unrealistically high expectations of what forensic science can achieve.

**2001**
Toxicologists examine a lock of hair that belonged to the French emperor Napoleon I, who died in 1821. It reveals that he suffered from long-term arsenic poisoning, which may have killed him.

**2006**
Automated Numberplate Recognition (ANPR) systems can now scan license plates at around one per second on vehicles traveling up to 100 mph (160 kmh). Using specialized CCTV cameras, ANPR reads the registration number and checks it on a database of stored license plates to identify the vehicle's owner.

# Find out more

FORENSIC SCIENCE IS BECOMING increasingly popular, especially among young people. It has long been represented in books and TV, but now it is getting interactive, too—in museum exhibitions and on special websites. For budding forensic scientists, or anyone with an interest in forensics, there are plenty of opportunities to explore this fascinating subject.

## USEFUL WEBSITES

- This site showcases forensic science resources for children and young adults
http:// www.all-about-forensic-science.com/science-for-kids

- Try some forensic science experiments and activities designed for children
http://www.hometrainingtools.com/articles/forensic-science-projects

- *Science News'* online magazine for 9–14-year-olds details the various fields of forensic science, and the inventions that made them possible
http://www.sciencenewsforkids.org/articles/20041215/Feature1.asp.

- Solve a make-believe crime and discover how you can practice forensic science at home
http://pbskids.org/dragonflytv/show/forensics.html

- London's Natural History Museum challenges the user to solve age-old crimes and mysteries using modern forensic science
http://www.nhm.ac.uk/nature-online/science-of-natural-history/forensic-sleuth

- *The CSI Experience: Web Adventure* has various games and activities based on the popular TV program
http://forensics.rice.edu/html/onlineactivities.html

Part of an interactive exhibition called "Please Identify Yourself!"

### FORENSICS ON SHOW
This is an exhibit from an exploration of biometrics at London's Science Museum. The exhibition explores the ways that new technology, such as computer face recognition, is increasingly used for identification.

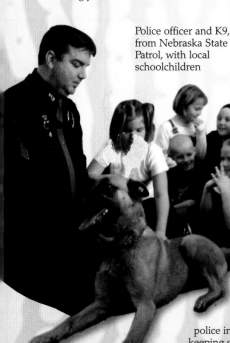

Police officer and K9, from Nebraska State Patrol, with local schoolchildren

### POLICE AT SCHOOL
In many parts of the world, police officers make educational visits to local schools. They may inform children about the role of the police in their community, and offer advice on keeping safe and asking for help when needed.

A museum guard dressed as a Victorian "bobby"

### MUSEUM OF DETECTION
In London's Baker Street, the Sherlock Holmes Museum pays tribute to that fictional master of "deductive reasoning"—using observation and logic to deduce specific information about a person's habits and lifestyle. The famous study is kept exactly as it is described in the stories.

# Glossary

### ACCELERANT
A highly flammable substance that can be used to start a fire, such as gasoline.

### ANTHROPOMETRY
A series of body measurements that was used by police forces for criminal identification before fingerprinting.

A bullet hole in reinforced glass leaves a clear record for the ballistics investigator

### ARCH
The rarest of fingerprint patterns. Only around five percent of fingerprint patterns are arches.

### ARSON
The crime of starting a fire deliberately in order to cause damage to property.

### AUTOPSY
A medical examination of a corpse in order to discover the cause of death. Also known as a postmortem.

### BALLISTICS
In forensic science ballistics means the study of guns, bullets, and trajectories. In general use, the word may be used to describe the science of the flight of projectiles.

### BLACK BOX
An event recorder, installed in planes, ships, and trains, that holds instrument and voice recordings, to be played in the event of a crash.

### BLOOD GROUP
Everyone belongs to one of four main blood groups: A, B, AB, or O. A test determines which group a sample belong to.

### CALIBER
Used as a measure of the inside diameter of a gun's barrel. Measurements may be inches, hundredths of inches, or millimeters.

### CARTRIDGE CASE
A cylinder containing the explosive charge and the bullet or pellets for a gun.

### CAUSE OF DEATH
The action that resulted in death (such as a blow to the head), as distinct from a medical condition (such as brain hemorrhage).

### CHAIN OF CUSTODY
The trail followed from crime scene to court by a piece of evidence held by the police and forensic scientists. Written records must show who passed the evidence to whom and when.

### CHROMATOGRAPHY
A series of laboratory tests designed to separate out the components of a mixture. In forensic science, chromatographic tests are used to discover the presence of drugs or poisons.

### CLEANSUIT
Outfit worn by forensic investigators at at crime scene, designed to prevent contamination.

### COMPARATOR
A device that enlarges and projects images of two different fingerprints for easy comparison.

### COMPARISON MICROSCOPE
A double microscope for examining two similar items, often bullets, side by side.

### COMPUTER TOMOGRAPHY (CT)
A method of X-raying the body in sections and creating three-dimensional images of its parts.

### DATABASE
An organized collection of information—such as DNA, fingerprints, or firearms—usually computerized for quick and easy searching.

### DUSTING
Brushing for latent fingerprints with a powder to make them visible.

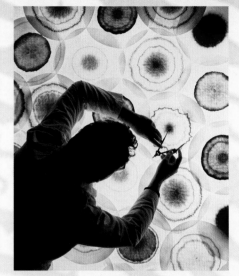

Scientist examining paper chromatograms

### E-FIT SYSTEM
Computerized version of the photographic identification system that uses photographs of facial features to create a likeness of a suspect. A similar system called FACES exists in the United States.

### ELECTROPHORESIS
Analytical method using an electric charge to grade substances by size and, in the case of DNA samples, generate DND profiles.

### ELECTROSTATIC DETECTION APPARATUS (ESDA)
A device that reveals handwriting impressions on paper with static electricity and toner.

### ENTOMOLOGY
The study of insects. A forensic entomologist studies the life cycles of insects found on corpses as an aid to estimating time of death.

### EVIDENCE MARKER
At a crime scene, used for marking the location of key evidence and identifying any special features.

## DNA—THE LADDER OF LIFE

Inside the nuclei of the cells that make up the different parts of our bodies is a spiral molecule called deoxyribonucleic acid, or DNA. It is a microscopic map of a person's unique features and characteristics, and a set of instructions for their development. The shape of DNA is often called the double helix, and it is composed of two strands that twist around each other. These are linked by rungs, which are composed of four different chemicals, shown here in different colors. It is the order of these chemical rungs that is different in every person—except for identical twins, triplets, and so forth, who are the only people on the planet to share the same DNA.

Model of the DNA double helix

*Each rung composed of two chemicals*

*Uncoiled, a DNA strand is 6 ft (2 m) long*

**FIBER EVIDENCE**
Evidence provided by human and animal hairs, or by synthetic fibers.

**FINGERTIP SEARCH**
A crime scene search carried out by several officers kneeling shoulder-to-shoulder.

**FORENSIC ANTHROPOLOGY**
The study of skeletons for identification. A forensic anthropologist typically tries to identify the victims of wars or major accidents when many are killed.

**GUNSHOT RESIDUE (GSR)**
Miscroscopic powder from explosive that is sprayed onto the hand of a person firing a gun. It is invisible, but can be detected with a hand swab up to six hours after firing.

**HOMICIDE**
The act of killing an individual. Can be manslaughter or murder.

**LARVA**
A stage in the development of an insect just before it undergoes metamorphosis. If larvae are found on a corpse, knowledge of their life cycle can help to indicate time of death.

**LASER BEAM**
An intense beam of monochromatic light. In forensic science, laser beams may be used at a crime scene to trace a bullet's trajectory.

**LATENT FINGERPRINT**
One that is not visible and requires special techniques to make it clear.

**LIE DETECTOR**
See Polygraph.

**LINEN TESTER**
An alternative magnifying glass often used by forensic investigators.

**LOCARD'S EXCHANGE PRINCIPLE**
The principle behind trace evidence collection and analysis—"every contact leaves a trace"—formulated by Edmond Locard.

**LOOP**
The most common fingerprint pattern, making up between 60 and 70 percent of fingerprints.

**LUMINOL**
A chemical spray used by forensic investigators to show up traces of blood. It can reveal years-old bloodstains.

**MAGNETIC WAND**
Used in conjunction with magnetic powder to dust for fingerprints on glossy surfaces.

**MASS SPECTROMETRY**
A technique used to measure very small amounts of substances, such as drugs, or to identify the presence of accelerants.

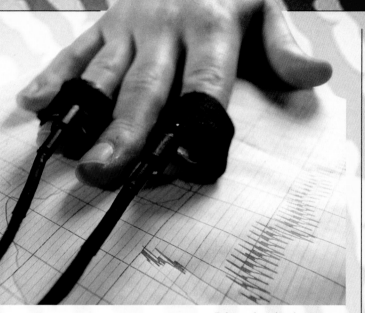

Polygraph or lie-detector test

**MORTUARY**
Also called a morgue, this is the place where dead bodies are kept before a funeral.

**ODONTOLOGY**
Forensic dentistry. This usually involves making identifications from bite marks, or matching a body's teeth to dental records.

**PARAMEDIC**
A person trained to give emergency medical treatment, often at a crime scene.

**PATHOLOGY**
The study of diseases from body tissue. A forensic pathologist examines suspicious deaths, and seeks to discover the cause of death by carrying out an autopsy.

**PATTERN EVIDENCE**
Evidence that is significant for its shape or pattern—in particular, bloodstains, which are classified in six different patterns.

**POLYGRAPH**
An instrument designed to discover whether a person is lying by recording changes in their blood pressure and pulse rate.

**POLYMERASE CHAIN REACTION (PCR)**
A method of duplicating fragments of DNA, until there is enough for DNA profiling or other analysis.

**POSTMORTEM INTERVAL**
The estimated time since death. *Post mortem* means "after death." See also Autopsy.

**PRECIPITIN TEST**
A test to distinguish human from animal blood.

**PRESUMPTIVE TEST**
A test, most commonly the Kastle-Meyer test, to show quickly whether a liquid is blood and therefore requires more detailed analysis.

**PROVENANCE**
A record of an object's history, including its origin and all of its owners. Important art and antiquities, provenance can be faked by forgers.

**RIFLING**
The raised, spiraling pattern in a gun barrel, which can cause distinctive marks on bullets.

**RIGOR MORTIS**
The stiffness of a corpse that occurs some hours after death. It can help investigators determine time of death.

**SCANNING ELECTRON MICROSCOPE (SEM)**
A powerful microscope that uses a beam of electrons instead of light to magnify an image.

**SEARCH PATTERN**
An organized method of searching a crime scene. There are many different search patterns.

**SEROLOGY**
The study of blood and other body fluids, usually for purposes of identification

**SNIFFER DOG**
A dog that has been trained to use its sensitive sense of smell to detect explosives, illegal drugs, missing people, or corpses.

**SUSPECT**
Someone who may be involved in a crime but who has not been formally charged.

**TAPE LIFT**
A method for recovering trace evidence—such as gunshot residue, fibers, or fingerprints—from a surface using adhesive tape.

**TOOLMARK**
Mark on a surface from which investigators may be able to identify the type of tool that made it, or even the individual tool.

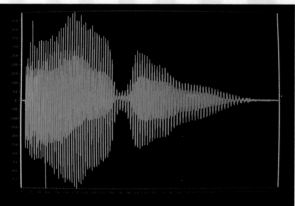

Voiceprint of a two-syllable word

**TOXICOLOGY**
The study of drugs and poisons.

**TRACE EVIDENCE**
Small objects or small amounts of substances that can be used as evidence—typically hair, fibers, or soil, transferred unknowingly by contact.

**VOICEPRINT**
Graphic representation of the sound of an individual's speech patterns, which may be used for identification.

**X-RAY**
A type of radiation used to scan and create an image of bones.

# Index

## AB

Abagnale, Frank, 64
accelerants, fires, 48, 50
aircraft crashes, 11, 52–53
Almodovar, Louise, 27
animals, DNA analysis, 23
anthrax, 40
anthropologists, forensic, 42–43
antimony, 41
arson, 48, 50
artworks, forgeries, 60–61
autopsy, 7, 38–39
bags, for evidence, 14, 15
ballistics, 32–33
Balthazard, Victor, 64
banknotes, 58
Bass, Dr. William, 35
behavior, profiling, 46–47
Bell, Joseph, 64
Bertillon, Alphonse, 8–9, 64
biometric ID, 62
birds, 23, 40
"black boxes," 52
blood, 20–21, 22, 39
blowflies, 36–37
body: at crime scene, 11, 13
  cause of death, 7, 38–39
  decomposition, 35, 36
  locating, 35
  skeleton, 42–43
Body Farm, 35, 37
bombs, 53, 54–55
bones, 42–43
brain, autopsy, 38, 39
brushes, fingerprint, 16
Brussel, Dr James A., 47
bullets, 30, 31, 32–33, 38
Buncefield oil depot, 49
burglars, 28, 46

## C

cameras, CCTV, 44, 45, 63
cannabis, 41
carbon dating, 59
carbon powder, 16, 17
carpet fibers, 26
cars: burned-out, 37
  crash investigations, 52
  paint, 24
  taking fingerprints, 16
  tracking, 63
  tire tracks, 28
cartridges, guns, 31, 32, 33
casts, 13, 28, 29
CCTV cameras, 44, 45, 63
cell phones, 56
cleansuits, 6, 11, 12–13
clothing: cleansuits, 6, 11, 12–13
  fibers, 27

comparator, fingerprints, 19
comparison microscopes, 24, 26, 33
computers: computer forensics, 56–57
  fingerprint matching, 19
  identifying suspects, 44
cone calorimeter, 50
corpse see body
Cottingley fairies, 61
crash investigations, 52–53
Crick, Francis, 22, 64
crime scene, 6, 10–11, 12–13
Crippen, Dr, 40, 64
CT scans, 43

## DEF

databases, 18, 23, 28, 62, 63
Dead Sea Scrolls, 59
death, cause of, 7, 38–39
decomposition, 35, 36
detective stories, 7, 8, 9
digital photography, 14
divers, 35
DNA analysis, 22–23, 39, 63, 64
documents, 58–59
dogs, sniffer, 34, 54
Doyle, Sir Arthur Conan, 9, 61
Dräger tube, 48
drugs, 34, 39, 40, 41
"dum-dum" bullets, 31
dummies, crash, 52
dust, 26
dynamite, 54
E-FIT system, 45
eggs, insect, 36, 37
electron microscopes, 24–25, 26, 32
electrophoresis, 23
electrostatic device, 59
endangered species, 23
entomologists, forensic, 36–37
environmental toxins, 40
ethnic differences, skulls, 42
exchange principle, 24, 27
explosions, 54–55
eyes, iris scanning, 62
faces: classifying, 8
  identifying, 44–45
  mapping, 63
  reconstruction, 43
Federal Bureau of Investigation (FBI), 6, 7, 46, 64
fiber samples, 26–27
fingerprints, 16–17, 18–19, 21
fingertip search, 11
firearm discharge residue, 30, 32
fires, 42, 48–49, 50–51
flies, 36–37
footprints, 13, 18, 21, 28, 29
forgeries, 58, 59, 60–61
future forensic science, 62–63

## GHI

Galton, Sir Francis, 18, 19, 64
Galton details, fingerprints, 19
gases, poisonous, 48, 50
genetic fingerprinting, 22–23
geographical profiling, 46
Glaister, Sir John, 20, 21, 64
Goddard, Calvin, 64
"golden hour," 10
grass seeds, 27
graves, 42
Gross, Hans, 64
ground-penetrating radar, 35
gunpowder, 54
guns, 6, 30–31, 32–33
gunshot residue, 30, 33
hackers, computer, 56
hair, 22, 25, 26, 39
hand prints, 17
handling evidence, 14–15
handwriting, 58, 59
Hauptmann, Bruno, 64
helicopters, 34
heroin, 41
Herschel, Sir William, 18, 65
history, 8–9
Hitler, Adolf, 59
Holmes, Sherlock, 9, 69
Hoover, J. Edgar, 9, 65
IAFIS, 64
identifying suspects, 44–45
identikit photos, 44
implants, 62
infrared light, 60, 63
insects, 36–37
internet, 56, 57
iris scanning, 62

## JKL

Jack the Ripper, 9
Jeffreys, Sir Alec, 22, 65
Kastle-Meyer test, 20–21
Keating, Tom, 60, 64
Kennedy, John F., 31, 47
KGB, 64
laboratories, 6, 9
Lacassagne, Alexandre, 65
Landsteiner, Dr. Karl, 20, 65
larvae, insect, 36–37
lasers, 19, 33, 43, 62
letters, 9
lie detectors, 8, 46, 47, 62
lifting tape, 16, 17
linen tester, 18
Locard, Dr. Edmond, 12, 24, 26, 27, 65
Lombroso, Cesare, 8

## MNO

"Mad Bomber," 47
maggots, 36, 37

magnetic wands, 17
magnifying glasses, 16
marker cards, 13
Markov, Georgi, 41, 65
Marsh, James, 65
mass spectrometry, 41
materials, fire testing, 50–51
measuring scales, 14
Metropolitan Police, 30
microchips, 57
microscopes, 8, 24–25, 26, 32, 33
missing-person searches, 34–35
molecules, 41
mortuary, 39
mugshots, 9
mushrooms, poisonous, 41
natural clues, 26–27
novels, 7, 8, 9
Operation Trident, 30
Orfila, Mathieu, 8, 65
organs, autopsy, 38
Osborn, Albert Sherman, 65
Oswald, Lee Harvey, 31, 47
oxygen, fires, 50, 51

## P

paint, 24
paintings, forgeries, 60–61
palmprints, 18
paper trails, 58–59
Parker, Ellis, 65
pathologists, forensic, 7, 38
Penry, Jacques, 44
phoneticians, forensic, 45
photographs: autopsy, 39
  crime scene, 12
  of evidence, 14
  faked, 61
  identification kits, 44
  mugshots, 9
pistols, 30, 31
plants, pollen, 26
poisons, 8, 40–41
pollen, 26
polygraph, 46, 47
postmortem examinations, 38–39
presumptive tests, 20–21
printers, 58
profilers, 46–47
psychologists, forensic, 46

## R

radar, 35
records, 12–13
Reichs, Kathy, 7
replica bullets, 31
ricin, 41
rifles, 30–31
robberies, 46
rollers, fingerprint, 16, 17
Rubenstein, "Big Mike", 35
Ruby, Jack, 47

## S

saliva, DNA analysis, 22
scales, 14
Scotland Yard, 65
sculptors, forensic, 42
searches, 11, 34–35
Shipman, Dr Harold, 56
shoes, footprints, 13, 18, 21, 28, 29
shotguns, 31
Simpson, O.J., 7
skeletons, 42–43
sketches, 12
skid marks, 52
skin flakes, 26
skull and crossbones, 40
skulls, 42, 43
slides, 26
smart cards, 57
smoke, from fires, 50
sniffer dogs, 34, 54
sonar equipment, 35
spectrometry, 27
speech, identifying suspect, 45
spontaneous combustion, 48
stab wounds, 38, 39
Starrs, James E., 65
static plates, 13
strychnine, 41
suicide bombers, 55
super-glue fuming, fingerprints, 19
Sûreté Nationale, 65

## TUVWX

teeth, 42
television, 7, 46
terrorism, 6, 40, 45, 54–55
thermoluminescence, 61
tissue analysis, 39
tool marks, 24, 28
tools, 14, 28, 38
toxicologists, forensic, 8, 40–41
trace evidence, 24–25
train crashes, 52, 53
trials, 9
Turin Shroud, 61
typewriters, 58
tire tracks, 28
Uhlenhuth, Paul, 20, 65
ultraviolet light, 28, 58
vacuum cleaners, 24
Van Meegeren, Han, 60
viruses, computer, 57
voiceprints, 45
Vucetich, Juan, 65
"Washington Sniper," 47
Watson, James, 22, 65
weapons, 30–31, 39
witnesses, 10, 44–45
wounds, 38, 39
writing, 58, 59
X-rays, 60

# Acknowledgments

**Dorling Kindersley would like to thank**
Peter Winfield for illustrations 11br, 32bc;
Stewart J. Wild for proofreading; Hilary Bird for the
index; David Ekholm-JAlbum, Sunita Gahir, Susan
St. Louis, Carey Scott, Lisa Stock, & Bulent Yusuf
for the clip art; Jim Green & Carey Scott for the
wall chart.

The publisher would like to thank the following
for their kind permission to reproduce their
photographs:

(key: a=above b=below/bottom c=center f=far
l=left r=right t=top)

**Alamy Images:** Si Barber 29tl; John Boykin 47br;
Scott Camazine 36crb; Jon Challicom 54bl; Chris
Gomersall 40tr; GOwst 69br; Mikael Karlsson 57tl,
69bl; Ellen McKnight 27b; Ian Miles-Flashpoint
Pictures 13cl, 13tl; Pablo Paul 12c, 28c; Pictorial
Press Ltd 56tl; Stocksearch 62ftl; Gari Wyn
Williams 13ca; Doug Wilson 52cl; **Ardea:** Pascal
Goetgheluck 37cl; Steve Hopkin 36tr, 37bc, 37cr,
37t; **CEPHOS Corporation:** 62bl; **Corbis:** 8cr, 31tr,
47cr; Lewis Allen 6tr; Morton Beebe 37br;
Annebicque CS Ltd 24tr; Bettmann 20tr, 27tr,
31tl, 33bl, 47tl, 64-65br; 65t; Régis Bossu/Sygma
53br; Andrew Brookes 68tr; Chesapeake City
Sheriffs Department/Reuters 47tc; Richard Chung/
Reuters 19br; John Mc Coy 47br; P. Deliss/Godong
61l; Kieran Doherty/Reuters 56cla; epa 49cr; **FDNY/
Assignment ID:** 30039450A 48tr; Federal Bureau
of Investigation/epa 46l; Laurence Fordyce/Eye
Ubiquitous 40tl; Hulton-Deutsch Collection 8cra,
40br; Nadeem Khawer/epa 55br; Micro Discovery
68l; Christopher J. Morris 7bc; Richard T. Nowitz
65b; Sebastian Pfuetze/zefa 7tl; Matt Rainey/Star
Ledger 7cl; Reuters 40bl, 40c, 41, 52-53t, 54c, 54cr,
54tr, 56cr, 63tr; Ron Sachs/CNP 47tr; Lucas Schifres
57tr; Scotland Yard/Reuters 45bl; Sion Touhig 54-
55tc; West Semitic Research/Dead Sea Scrolls
Foundation 59tr; Tim Wright 52bl; **Courtesy of
The Bank of England:** 58b; **The Design Works,
Sheffield:** 38cl, 38cr, 38tc, 38tl, 38tr; **DK Images:**
Courtesy of HM Customs and Excise 4fcl, 34ca;
Courtesy of the Metropolitan Police Museum,
London 4cl, 8-9ca, 8-9t, 9tr; **Dr Thomas
Heseltine/Aurora CS Ltd:** 63tl; Dr Thomas
Heseltine 44br; **The Electronic Frontier
Foundation:** 58tr; **Environmental Criminology
Research Inc.:** 46cra, 46tr; **Faro UK:** Neil Barnett
43cl; **Firearmsid.com:** 31br; **www.firetactics.com:**
48b; **Foster & Freeman Ltd.:** 28br; **Granada
Television Limited:** 46br; **The Kobal Collection:**
CBS-TV 7cr; Dreamworks 64-65l; Universal 9bl;
**Lexis Public Relations:** 69t; **London Fire
Brigade:** 48cr; **Mary Evans Picture Library:** 48br;
Chris Coupland 66t; **Missouri State Police Crime
Laboratory:** 28tr; **PA Photos:** 10-11b, 11ca, 11cl,
11cr, 34tr, 34-35b, 35tl, 39br, 41bl, 42c, 42tl, 42tr,
56br, 60l; Gareth Copley 35c; Ian Nicholson/PA
Archive 30tl; **Photoshot:** UPPA 20cl; **Reuters:** John
Sommers II 35tc; **Rex Features:** 55bc, 55cl;
**Science Photo Library:** A. Barrington Brown 22cl;
Dr Tony Brain 26bl; Dr Jeremy Burgess 70l; CNRI
42cr; Charles D.Winters 45br; Michael Donne 49t;
Mauro Fermariello 24tl, 29r; E. Gueho 26crb; James
King-Holmes 61bc, 62-63bl; Mark Maio/King-
Holmes 62br; Peter Menzel 6-7bl; Hank Morgan
71b; Louise Murray 35br; Susumu Nishinaga 26br;
David Parker 22bl; Pasieka 66-67 (Background), 68-
69 (Backdrop), 68-69 (Background), 70-71
(Background); Philippe Psaila 33br, 33cl, 33cr;
David R.Frazier 16tr; David Scharf 26clb; Science
Source 67b; Volker Steger 60b; Tek Image 20c, 63br,
71t; Geoff Tompkinson 70tr; Volker Steger, Peter
Arnold Inc. 24tr; **www.skullsunlimited.com:**
42bl, 42cl, 42clb; **TopFoto.co.uk:** 9c, 60t, 65c;
Fortean 61t; **VisionMetric Ltd:** 45cl, 45cr, 45t; **The
Wellcome Institute Library, London:** 8bc, 8c,
8fcl; **Susan Moberly:** 23bc; **Jerry Young:** 43t

**Wall Chart: PA Photos:** John Giles / PA Archive
ca (fingertip search); **The Wellcome Institute
Library, London:** Susan Moberly clb (DNA
profiles)

**Jacket:** *Front:* **PA Photos:** Chris Young (b).
**Punchstock:** Digital Vision/John Lamb (tcr).
**Science Photo Library:** TEK Image (tl); National
Library of Medicine (tr); Philippe Psaila (tcl). *Back:*
**Corbis:** Ashley Cooper (b); Image 1 (cr). **Science
Photo Library:** Michael Donne, University of
Manchester (tr); Volker Sleger, Peter Arnold Inc.
(cl).

All other images © Dorling Kindersley
For further information see: **www.dkimages.com**